The Pitched Roof

The Pitched Roof
Architecture Manual

Barbara Burren Martin Tschanz Christa Vogt Eds.
ZHAW Zentrum Konstruktives Entwerfen

Niggli

Editors
Barbara Burren, Martin Tschanz and Christa Vogt
Zürcher Hochschule für Angewandte Wissenschaften
Zentrum Konstruktives Entwerfen, Winterthur

Conception and editing
Barbara Burren, Martin Tschanz and Christa Vogt

Text editing
Miriam Seifert-Waibel, Jonathan Styles

Translation from German
Lynette Widder

Layout
Urs Stuber, Frauenfeld

Typesetting
Daniela Bieri-Mäder, Niederbüren

Lithography and printing
Heer Druck AG, Sulgen

Binding
Buchbinderei Schumacher AG, Schmitten

ISBN 978-3-7212-0680-7

A special thank goes to our partners in the industry, who enabled and supported our research and the publication on hand.

Eternit®   **zzwancor**   **VELUX®**

zh aw Architektur, Gestaltung und Bauingenieurwesen
Zentrum Konstruktives Entwerfen

Preface

New Responsibilities for the Traditional School of Architecture in Winterthur

Stephan Mäder, Chair, Department of Architecture, Design and Civil Engineering, ZHAW

Swiss technical colleges have the responsibility, in addition to teaching, to offer research and development services and continuing education. The Department of Architecture, Design and Civil Engineering at the Zürcher Hochschule für Angewandte Wissenschaften (ZHAW, or Zurich University of Applied Sciences) pursues this responsibility consistently and uncompromisingly, particularly with the activities of the two Centers for Urban Landscape and Constructive Design.

The actual area of influence for architects and civil engineers is, however, practice. The induction of knowledge and competence to the pedagogic activity of the School in Winterthur is primarily achieved via practicing professionals. However, when several years ago the responsibility for research and development was also given to technical colleges as an extension of their offerings, this meant that, in addition to practice, the University of Applied Sciences in Winterthur needed to access broader areas of knowledge generation within its own facilities.

This demanding responsibility offers chances for the School's identity and profile. It also involves risks, such as latent pedagogic misdirection or supercilious fixation on fashionable topics. The expanded responsibility thus cannot be absorbed into hermetic research cells but must be executed on the point of intersection among teaching, research and practice in collaboration with interested partners from the public sector and industry.

At the School of Architecture in Winterthur, the two Centers for Urban Landscape and Constructive Design assume this responsibility. Their efforts achieve a close relationship between research and teaching. The Centers define the research topics and formulate appropriate complexes of questions. These are then, case by case, introduced into the design studio courses and the research modules of the Master's Degree program. By raising issues in an open manner, students can respond with design methods and with the formulation of innovative approaches to solutions based upon spatial constructs. Thus, the topic of the "pitched roof" and the "rooftop addition" were studied on repeated occasion in the design courses. The student work was perhaps a subordinate component in the preparation of the phased research project "The Pitched Roof" which was executed at the Center for Constructive Design of the ZHAW in collaboration with well-known partners from the industry. Nonetheless, the "unpolished gems" from the studios which can be refined further at the Center for Constructive Design comprise the foundation of the research projects and thus also for this publication. This is no less true even if only one of the essays focuses on an evaluation of the related design courses. The teaching component of the project has proven itself to be a truly experimental laboratory for innovative project ideas and their potential application in design processes.

Research at technical colleges is accomplished through project-specific financing. In other words, it is only possible to set aside financing in the operating budget for clearly defined projects. In addition, it is fundamental that all projects are supported by financial contributions from industry partners or the public sector. In theory, the most decisive principle at technical colleges is that only those projects will be approved that have been co-financed by external partners and therefore prove to be explicitly desired by them.

To an enquiry by the brick industry as to whether, given the large number of flat roof building in the Swiss construction industry, the School could assist in spurring increased sales, we were compelled to give a negative response. Their request could have best been answered by marketing or public relations. The basic impulse, however, led to a fundamental discussion on the role and meaning of the pitched roof in architecture, carried out at the Center for Constructive Design under the leadership of Matthias Bräm and Astrid Staufer. With the support of the industry partners Eternit, Velux and ZZ Wancor, a small team consisting of Barbara Burren, Martin Tschanz and Christa Vogt could work to study in depth and to represent the architectural and spatial potentials of the pitched roof. The investigation and evaluation of built examples contributed to a largely undiscovered and un-interpreted treasure trove for contemporary architectural production.

The handbook entitled *The Pitched Roof* summarizes the results of this intensive study. It is an example of the way in which the intersection of teaching, research and development, including service providing, can be worked upon to make a substantial contribution to the daily craft of the architect.

Walter Gropius, *Internationale Architektur* (Bauhaus books 1), Munich 1925, pp. 54 f.

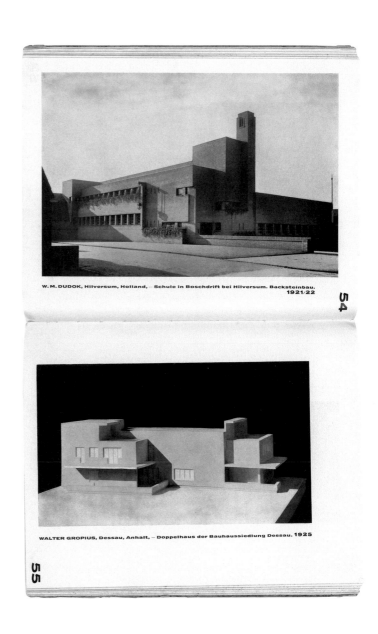

W. M. DUDOK, Hilversum, Holland, — Schule in Boschdrift bei Hilversum. Backsteinbau. 1921/22

54

WALTER GROPIUS, Dessau, Anhalt, — Doppelhaus der Bauhaussiedlung Dessau. 1925

55

Introduction

Barbara Burren, Martin Tschanz, Christa Vogt

For decades, the pitched roof has played at best, if at all, the role of architectural step-child. The identification of high-quality Modern architecture with the flat roof, already entrenched by the late 1920s, was always highly questionable, but it has redoubled its hold since the 1960s with increasing force. In singular cases, there were always periodically excellent, architecturally challenging implementations of the pitched roof, particularly in churches, large halls and houses. Nonetheless, it was, for example, quite possible in the 1980s to complete the study of architecture without once having considered the architecture of the roof.

In recent times, however, there has been a stronger interest in this topic. In 2006, the journal *werk, bauen + wohnen* published an issue on it[1] and one year later, the "Dortmunder Architekturtage" were devoted to the subject of the roof.[2] Many newer buildings prove that particularly younger architects, who have often been compelled to use pitched roofs by building codes, rediscover their potentialities and use them with gusto. In doing so, they can have recourse to the experience from the recent past, gathered outside the realm of traditional building practice. Both in the object-like architecture of the "monolith" or "bubble," and in an architecture that understands itself as the built continuation of the topography, the exterior surfaces arch or fold themselves – and beneath them, spaces are generated which often have the explicit character of the space beneath the roof, although from the exterior, there is nothing to evoke a traditional roof. It thus becomes obvious that the traditional terms are at their limits.[3]

Pitched Roofs

We have in this case decided to employ a pragmatic definition of the pitched roof. It includes all surfaces containing a building's uppermost perimeter as long as they are not horizontal. This definition is simple and clear. Beyond that, it permits the creation of a relationship between traditional roofs and newer forms of hulls and envelopes. This elucidates issues on both sides, both the comprehension of new forms and the understanding of presumably well-known roofs. Many topics, problems and possibilities are common to both areas, if in modified forms. As a kind of corrective measure, we have excluded from our considerations those flat roofs that had such primacy in Modern architecture. In this way, we hope to sharpen sensitivity to all the possibilities, which are opened once the automatic recourse to the flat roof is contravened. In the course of work, it was also clear that the flat roof could be seamlessly integrated into these examples as a special case.

The book is directed to working architects with the goal of presenting the broad spectrum of effects which can be achieved using the pitched roof. This goal corresponds to the book's structure, which has as a consequence the fact that such important topics as construction do not have their own chapter, but rather are allowed to play a role in a variety of contexts. The chapters concentrate initially on the nature of the effect *within* and *upon* the exterior space, then *within* and *upon* the interior space, both of which have hardly been discussed prior to now. An important component is located between these two, which describes the relationship between inside and outside. This has gained meaning since the space between the roof, which traditionally often had a subordinate function as poché, is today usually a functional or even a major space in its own right. The interplay between interior and exterior appearance of the roof is therefore correspondingly important, similar to that always attributed to the façade.

Images and Texts

In this handbook, images play an essential role. It follows the tradition of the "picture book" in the sense of those that formed the architecture of Modernism.[4] Here, however, it is not a case of providing the "fast reader"[5] with quickly consumable information. Our compendium also does not reflect the intention to illustrate or even to prove the rectitude of a claim with a collection of similar images, as did, for example, the photographs in Walter Gropius's first Bauhaus book, which was intended to demonstrate the internationality and stylistic specificity of Modern architecture.[6]

Werner Lindner/Georg Steinmetz, *Die Ingenieurbauten in ihrer guten Gestaltung*, Berlin 1923, p. 40f.
Bernard Rudofsky, *Architecture Without Architects*, New York 1966, p. 143f.

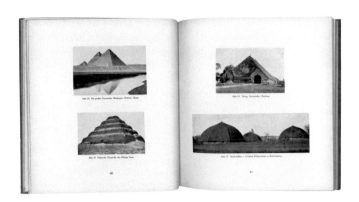

It is much more important to us that the images be compared in a way that allows a topic to emerge from looking at the plates together, as a *Tertium Comparationis*. In some cases, it will emerge through similarities, but mostly through differences, so that a spectrum of forms becomes clear simultaneously with each theme.

"The comparison says much without words, it even makes the mute loquacious," as Paul Brandt stated in the 1910 preface to his art historical best seller *Sehen und erkennen*.[7] Nonetheless, we did not want to forego words with our comparative images. Captions offer assistance in seeing and make the corresponding topic explicit, so that the plausibility of the pictorial argument can be tested. Of course we hope for ourselves that the comparison "speaks immediately from the image to the eye and heart"[8] and yet also, that reason is involved, too. The incongruities among images which often derive from different periods and contexts is by no means a disadvantage; on the contrary, "precisely where such connections are impossible, that is where the laws inherent to art present themselves even more clearly,"[9] as Brandt concluded.

We look with admiration upon such books as *Die Ingenieurbauten in ihrer guten Gestaltung* by Werner Lindner and Georg Steinmetz,[10] *Architecture Without Architects* by Bernard Rudofsky,[11] or the famous comparative images framed by Sigfried Giedion, for example in his classic *Space, Time and Architecture*.[12] The reproach that these are unserious or even manipulate would only be true if their goal had been to do justice to the photograph's subjects beyond the aspects described by the comparison. Giedion's juxtaposition of Francesco Borromini's dome of Sant'Ivo della Sapienza with a sculpture by Pablo Picasso, for example, might be condemned by the rules of art history as "irritating, unacceptable and absolutely frivolous."[13] Nonetheless, it can, beyond the boundaries of discipline and era, focus attention on the possibility of permitting surfaces to engage space by means of their sculptural modulation and to link geometry and imagination.[14]

In our plates, too, the images may of course not comprehensively describe the roofs they show, much less the entire buildings. We even include certain images which may convey a misleading impression by means of a particular view, if it were a matter of the entire building itself.

The dissolution of the bond between image and context is the price paid for the clarity of the statement made possible by the newly formed context. On the other hand, it is important that images are more than mere illustrations of predetermined contexts. Our work was, simultaneously and in parallel, a seeking and a gathering of images, just as it was a finding and a refining of topics. Even in the final result, the images and the captions retain mutual independence: the consideration of the images influences the reading of the short texts and vice versa.

We believe that the working method to which we refer will meet the architect halfway. Architects are accustomed to working with references which they apply in the design process[15] and, at least to a point, betray.[16] Our plates offer themselves expressly for this purpose. In comparison to an analytical text, they are immeasurably more open. They are characterized more by their inspiring capacity to suggest than by an attempt at comprehensive and final explanation. The knowledge, which emanates from them proves to be a possibility which opens new perspectives.[17]

Allied to this strength is equally the weakness that accrues to the argumentation deployed by the plates. Analytical focus and definitiveness can only be achieved inadequately with this structure, and even less so, an appropriate representation of complexity. But to do without these would be highly dissatisfying. Thus, the annotated collection of images in each chapter is complimented by an essay in which one aspect is culled and discussed in depth. We have consciously permitted differing methodical and content-based approaches to come to the fore, as a way of demonstrating the scope of the topic area. In any case, what is true of an interesting roof is as true of the work of architecture in general: that it, as a whole, integrates multiplicity in its form. It is a matter of exterior and interior, of space and prism, of the building itself and its context, of shelter and of an opening, of meaning and effect – and all of this together. Thus, in the final chapter, the perspective is reversed and a case study is used to interpret one chosen roof in its multivalent qualities.

This handbook on the architecture of the pitched roof cannot and does not want to present in its sum total a comprehensive, conclusive theory. Nonetheless, we hope that this prolegomena offers an enlightening and inspiring contribution to this topic. We could, for our part, build upon the experiences that we have gathered over the past five years at the "Center for Constructive Design" at the Zurich University of Applied Sciences in Winterthur. Our work was accompanied and, in that form, ultimately made possible by the administration of the Department of Architecture, Design and Civil Engineering at the Zurich University of Applied Sciences, and by our partners in industry: Eternit, Velux and ZZ Wancor. The topic has proven to be absolutely inexhaustible and so interesting, that we found only sympathy amongst the authors we sought for our project. We offer our heartfelt thanks to them all.

1   *werk, bauen + wohnen*, "Das Dach", No. 4, 2006.
2   See *Dortmunder Architekturheft*, "Das Dach", No. 20, 2008.
3   The essay "Roof, House, Prism" (p. 36) discusses this item.
4   Werner Oechslin, "Das 'Bild': der (vordergründige) Konsens der Moderne?", in: Oechslin, *Moderne entwerfen – Architektur und Kulturgeschichte*, Cologne 1999, pp. 35–43 (first appeared in French in: *Faces*, No. 17, 1990, pp. 6–9; English in: *a+u*, No. 245, 1991, pp. 28–39).
5   Although Sigfried Giedion's preliminary notes in *Building in France* as quoted are entirely valid for this book: "This book is written and designed so that it is possible for the hurried reader to understand the developmental path from the captioned illustrations; the text furnishes closer explication …", Sigfried Giedion, *Building in France, Building in Ferro Concrete, Santa Monica*, CA 1995, translated by J. Duncan Berry, p. 83.
6   Walter Gropius, *Internationale Architektur*, Munich 1925.
7   Paul Brandt, *Sehen und erkennen* (Introduction to first edition 1910), Stuttgart 1968, S. V.
8   Ibid.
9   Ibid.

10 Werner Lindner/Georg Steinmetz, *Die Ingenieurbauten in ihrer guten Gestaltung*, Berlin 1923.
11 Bernard Rudofsky, *Architecture Without Architects*, New York 1964.
12 Sigfried Giedion, *Space, Time and Architecture*, Cambridge 1946.
13 See: Dorothee Huber, "Images parlantes – Sur la régie texte-image de Giedion", in: *Faces*, No. 17, 1990, pp. 10–15.
14 However Giedion does not make it easy for us, when in the caption he references as unifying element "the astonishing effect" on the contemporaries, which can not be deduced from the pictures alone (Siegfried Giedion, *Raum, Zeit, Architektur*, Ravensburg 1965, p. 95).
15 See: *werk, bauen + wohnen*, No. 10, 2005 ("Anverwandlung").
16 In his lectures at the ETH, Francesco W. Collotti often described the architect as "tradutore" und "traditore", as translator and traitor, simultaneously. See Francesco Collotti, *Architekturtheoretische Notizen*, Lucerne 2001.
17 On thinking and designing "in images, metaphors, models, analogies, symbols and allegories", see O. M. Ungers' introduction to his (picture) book *Morphologie – City Metaphors* (Cologne 1982).

Roof and Prism

Roof and Prism

If one considers the topic paraphrased by the terms "roof and prism," one's attention is trained on the relationship between substructure and roof, or on the form of the roof itself. In most cases, however, the two entities work together. A particular roof can lend a building orientation, centering or articulation. At the same time, roof and substructure can contribute mutually to their effect by melding in reciprocity to become a single figure. Or they can even meld into a prism in which any differentiation between roof and wall is simply absent.

As Martin Tschanz notes, certain fundamental questions about the validity of these concepts arises: "Can the point at which roof and wall meld really allow for the designation of a roof in its true sense? And on the other hand, can the point at which the two pieces remain independent be designated a prism? Is it not rather the case that the concepts 'prism' and 'roof' are mutually exclusive because they belong to entirely different conceptions of architecture?" In this essay, Tschanz propounds the thesis that a recognizable roof finally makes a house out of a building, whether the roof is pitched or flat. Of course pitched roofs have a different effect on human perception than do flat ones. Thus, pitched roofs – rather than horizontal ones – conjoin themselves optically with the adjacent wall planes to create a continuous hull, which reaches the ground plane. The reasons for this stem from the fact that wall and roof are visible simultaneously, and that the eye sees an obtuse angle as less of a caesura than it does a right angle or an acute one. In fact, the appearance of pitched roof edge can be sufficient to achieve a similar effect, "visual forces are not isolated vectors, but must be understood as components of perceptual fields that surround buildings."[1] Thus, the human eye tends to extend the angles of a gable to the ground, creating the impression that the building is firmly anchored to its location. This is in sharp contrast to a building with a flat roof, which, by virtue of the horizontal roof line, looks as if it could be moved at will.

Barbara Burren

---

1   Rudolph Arnheim, *The Dynamics of Architectural Form,* Berkeley 1977, p. 28.

Independent Roof

As demonstrated by the two houses in La Martella, whose gabled façades front the street, it is enough to include a small offset in order for a roof to be read as an independent element set atop the substructure. The roofs of the town houses in Tiburtino are partially set apart from the volume below by the loggia beneath, which is enveloped in shade – this recalls the open spaces beneath the roofs of traditional houses. At the same time, they are securely bound to the prism by the corner columns. In comparison, the roofs of the Robie House in Chicago, with their deep eaves, seem to levitate, defying gravity above the long ribbon windows. The building does not appear to be a solid volume but rather dissolves into different horizontal bands. In Le Corbusier's pavilion in Zurich, the roof stands alone. Its construction and its geometry, it is independent from the cubes beneath it.

Ludovico Quaroni **Housing Unit La Martella, Matera, 1954**
Ludovico Quaroni, Mario Ridolfi et al. **Town Houses Quartiere Tiburtino, Rome, 1954**
Frank Lloyd Wright **Frederick C. Robie House, Chicago, 1908**
Le Corbusier **Heidi Weber Pavilion, Zurich, 1967**

Roof as Prism

At night, the crystalline glass prisms atop the Kunsthaus in Glarus distinguish themselves from the building below as glowing lanterns, but during the day, both nearly meld into a compact volume. Contrary to this, the cantilevering roof volume in the Hanging Tower of Schönenwegen sits like a lid on the high timber shaft. In the country house in Knebworth, the gabled surfaces are articulated as part of the roof in their materiality and thus define the roof as a slightly cantilevered prism. The sculptural independence of the articulated roofscape creates a distinctive contrast to the base. This difference is even more obvious in Herning. Like sculptures, it's light catchers sit on the closed base which binds the lot together.

Hans Leuzinger   **Kunsthaus, Glarus, 1948**
Hanging Tower, Schönenwegen, ca. 1890
Edwin Lutyens   **Country House, Knebworth, 1901**
Jørn Utzon   **Private House, Herning, 1967**

Building as Prism

Hans Poelzig **Model House, Breslau, 1904**
BKK-3 **Miss Sargfabrik, Vienna, 2001**
Herzog & de Meuron **Rudin House, Leymen, 1997**
OMA **Casa da Música, Porto, 2005**

Roof and wall can approximate one another to the point at which it is no longer possible to speak of a roof in the strict sense. In the model house in Breslau, the roof material extends to the gable wall, which is unified with the drawn-down pitched roof. The aperture type, on the other hand, conforms to the traditional understanding of roof and wall. In the Miss Sargfabrik in Vienna, on the other hand, the façade becomes an all-encompassing hull; it is only the silhouette that "says" roof. In the Rudin House, too, roof and wall are made to look similar, although the roof remains incomparably more present because of the particular form of the house. In contrast, the concert house in Porto is a crystalline, monolithic prism comprised of equally important oblique planes; entirely self-referential, it no longer recalls the conventional image of a house.

Just Roof

A roof is enough to define a house. Like a stretched canopy, the roof protects the medieval digs without interrupting the continuity of the earth. In a similar manner, the broadly spanning shell, supported on only four points, defines a space at the garden center in Camorino, which is open on all sides to the surrounding plane. In the case of the student hous-ing in Stockholm, there is a completed building vol-ume but it disappears almost entirely in the shadow of the wide-spanning roof plane. The simple tent which the church at Rönsahl recalls, is a trusted originary form of a building that comprises no more than a roof.

Folds and Loops

Renzo Piano **Paul Klee Center, Bern, 2005**
Foreign Office Architects **Passenger Terminal, Yokohama, 2002**
Justo García Rubio **Bus Station, Cáceres, 2003**
smarch **New Apostolic Church, Zuchwil, 2005**

Buildings can be configured through the deformation of a continuous plane, in which case it is impossible to discern a clear difference between roof and wall, or to speak of a prism. Such buildings often attempt to recreate a natural landscape, or to create an artificial one. The former is true in case of the roof plane of the Klee Center in Bern, which follows the form of the gentle hills in the immediate landscape and, at the same time, nestles itself into them. The Yokohama Terminal, on the other hand, is an autonomous artificial landscape made of folded oblique planes, which can simultaneously be roof, wall or ramp. The bus station in Cáceres is formed from a continuous band which spans the bus stop as a roof and then is looped into a waiting room for passengers. The formation of space in the church at Zuchwil is more complex still, since there is no continuity in the bent surface. The space is contained by a number of interlaid warped floor and ceiling planes.

The roof form can lend a building a physiognomy, which can recall humans or animals. Such buildings invite description with concepts borrowed from anatomy, such as head, body or wings. They are often free standing so that their individual, characteristic form can be perceived as a whole.

The roof's form can center a building or give it an orientation. In the chapel at Valdemarsvik, in relation to the heavy, static base the dynamically upsweeping roof marks the building's middle, and thus indicates a clear locus within the broad cemetery complex. It is similar to the single-family house in Altendorf, although in this case, it is a hefty hipped roof which anchors the building as a whole and orients it to the interior despite the over-dimensioned windows which are arranged collage-like in the walls. On the other end of the spectrum, the high-pitched gabled roof of the Brusttuch House orients the building with its end façade to the plaza, whereas the side façades pick up the trajectories of the streets. The regionally typical gabled roof of the base station for the Nordkettenbahn funicular opens on one side to a shed roof so that the building is oriented towards the mid-way station with a forceful gesture.

Subdividing and Unifying

In the Amsterdam housing project Schwartzeplein, the architecture suggests gambrel roofs and thus a series of semi-attached but independent buildings with chimneys between them, although in plan the building is clearly recognizable as a single bar. The front façade of the Rappolt House in Hamburg is dominated by an imposing main gable, whereas its long side façade is articulated rhythmically by a row of smaller cross-gables. Seen from the street, they refer to the gable roof that cannot be seen from that vantage. The enormous volume of the shaft house of the copper mine in Hancock looks like a village comprised of many agglomerated single houses which are, then, unified by virtue of the vertical stepping. In the Sea Ranch housing project, the different houses appear to be a conglomerate because of the unified slope and materials.

Michel de Klerk, Pieter Kramer **Schwartzeplein Housing, Amsterdam, 1922**
Fritz Hoeger **Rappolt House, Hamburg, 1912**
Shaft House, Hancock, ca. 1850
Charles Moore et al. **Sea Ranch Housing, Sonoma County, 1965**

The First Building. Eugène-Emmanuel Viollet-le-Duc, *Histoire de l'habitation humaine depuis les temps préhistoriques jusqu'à nos jours*, Paris 1875, Fig. 2.

Jørn Utzon, Sketch of the Chinese House.

Roof, House, Prism

Martin Tschanz

The question of the relationship between roof and prism *(Baukörper)*[1] seems to be a simple and clear one, in which the spectrum of possibilities is quickly ascertained. An emphatically formulated gap can create a demonstrative separation between the two components which otherwise, as proven above all by more recent examples, could meld into one if the transition between the two is repressed. Somewhere between these extremes is the classical solution of a cornice, which relates and conjoins wall to roof without subverting their individuality.

And nonetheless, doubts remain. Can the point at which roof and wall meld really allow for the designation of a roof in its true sense? And on the other hand, can the point at which the two pieces remain independent be designated a prism? Is it not rather the case that the concepts "prism" and "roof" are mutually exclusive because they belong to entirely different conceptions of architecture?

Roof as Hat

In German etymology, the words "roof" *(Dach)* and "to cover" *(bedecken)* are so closely related that we implicitly understand that a roof's essential characteristic is to provide cover. Certainly there is also the word "covering" *(Decke,* which also means in German "ceiling" as well as "floor slab" and "blanket")* but such coverings can lie atop many things and may themselves be covered over again. A roof, however, forms the uppermost conclusion of a building. It is nonetheless a special subset of covers – a point of view already held by Leon Battista Alberti: "Of coverings some are open to the Air, others are not," as he noted tersely but precisely in his *10 Books of Architecture.*[2]

One may not expect a roof in an architectural sense to furnish this shelter, or separation between a safe place beneath and a place open to the sky above, not only in a technical sense but also demonstratively. A building that is "roofed" (meaning, too, in the German play on words, "conceived") in this way is what we call a house. In ancient Greek, "tegos" means both roof and house, and in German, too, the original meaning of the word "to cover" is incipient in both terms.[3] Correspondingly widespread in the history of architectural theory are legends of origin which claim that the first element of architecture was the roof.[4] It is therefore easy for us to imagine a house which consists only of a roof over one's head, whereas a house without a roof is difficult to imagine. In German, someone who is homeless is called "roofless."

The close kinship between the words "house" and "hat" *(Haus and Hut),* noted by Martin Heidegger,[5] supports this idea. It furthermore leads one to understand the roof/hat as a vessel which not only configures a beneath, but also forms a space and an interior: "beneath the roof" means "in a house" regardless of whether there are enclosing walls or not. A roof does not simply rest above the house, but rather, by virtue of its sheltering quality, comprises the house.[6]

As a hollow volume, it is comparable to a vessel such as a basin, a pitcher or a ship's hold, albeit in "upside-down" form, open at the bottom. As such, it permits the creation of an entirely different relationship to place. A boat, for example, usually seems to us to be defined and autonomous. Gravity presses one down into its belly, holds one within it as it separates one from the bottom of the sea; everything is poised to float away at any time. An overturned boat, on the other hand, whose hold becomes a roof, seems to us immeasurably more open: it is an invitation to crawl beneath it. The ground runs continuously beneath it but at the same time, is differentiated at the area beneath the boat by the shelter it offers.

Because a roof is essential to a house, we must recognize a building as roofed in order for us to accept it as a house. Therefore we do not necessarily need to see the sheltering roof membrane. Especially in the dense space of the inner city, it often eludes our view. Perhaps we might see its gable, which indicates the roof and its form within the street space.[7] Perhaps it is only the underside of an eaves or of a cornice that is the true or apparent extremity of a roof structure. In the Palazzo Farnese in Rome, for example, we intimate a shallowly sloped hipped roof, but it is impossible to verify this from the perspective of a pedestrian. Apparently it is not the form of the roof which is important but rather that we can recognize a roof as a powerful, independent element simply by virtue of its cornice. It tells us that beneath it, there is a well-sheltered interior space worth entering.

Prisms

In the famous flat-roof issue (1927) of the periodical *Das Neue Frankfurt,* Adolf Behne wrote that the flat roof "obliges us to return to a view of the building as a unified body."[8] Apparently, this statement is highly questionable. One needs only to think of Ludwig Mies van der Rohe's Barcelona Pavilion or Richard Neutra's villas, which are anything but unified bodies despite their flat roofs. Even the images which accompanied Behne's essay express a different thought: that it is not the shift from pitched to flat roof but rather the absence of an articulated roof that creates the desired effect of a unified body.

In this light, it is understandable that Henry Russell Hitchcock and Philip Johnson felt compelled to criticize in *The International Style* the quite modestly eaves of the Waterwork Houses in Zurich.[9] This is not a detail but on the contrary, precisely the element that makes the building neither a "unified body" or prism nor a pure volume, but rather, a house in the sense denoted above. This was in fact at stake in an exchange that claimed to be about the issue of flat or pitched roofs: whether a building was to be read as house or furthermore as volume or prism. As a house, it spans between above and below and orients itself accordingly; it is also, given its continuity with the ground, fundamentally open. Otherwise, it is an isotropic, autonomous construct. Adolf Behne's formulation of house as unified prism seems, in this light, an oxymoron.

The cubic block so preferred by Modern architecture is, for an architecture which defines itself as "the masterly, correct and magnificent play of masses brought together in light,"[10] ultimately an inappropriate form – at least if the laws of human perception are to be considered. Its three-dimensionality is first perceptible seen on the oblique or in motion, whereas it appears flat and entirely non-spatial seen frontally. "A flat roof, however, hides the top face of a building from anybody who is looking up to it, and therefore the stark roof line of such a building tends to make it look flat, like a sheet of paper," as Rudolf Arnheim concluded appropriately. And furthermore, "a pitched roof, apart from its practical functions, continues the shape of the building beyond the frontal plane; it makes it either the depth dimension and thereby helps to define it for the eyes as a solid."[11] We first see it as a prism in the strict sense if its surfaces no longer essentially differ from one another, so that there is no longer an articulated roof or façade plane in the true sense. This can be achieved in a roof-less, flatly spanned building by withholding this knowledge from perception so that the eye completes the volume by analogy to the visible surfaces. Alternately, it can also be achieved by forming all surfaces in the same way. Compact constructs formed of many polygonal or continuously curved surfaces seem particularly object-like because their three-dimensional entirety is immediately comprehensible, as Arnheim describes. Whether such a building is understood as formed by "smooth surfaces, which circumscribe a space"[12] or as a solid volume is in fact immaterial to perception. One way or another, we experience it as a compact, self-referential vis-à-vis[13] whose relationship to the place on which it stands remains unstable. Its ancestor is not the primitive hut but rather the box or stone that was first located in a primitive gesture to form the first monument.

Roof Volume

The worlds of prisms and of houses are not so clearly distinguishable from each other as the preceding differentiation might perhaps suggest. One the one hand, roofs themselves can often appear explicitly prismatic, and on the other, we often perceive structures to be roofed although they have no roof in an architectural sense.

Because of their sheltering function, roofs are primarily constituted of closed, compact, homogeneous surfaces whereas the areas

**Bild 10: BAUBLOCK DER GEHAG=SIEDLUNG
BERLIN=BRITZ. Architekt Bruno Taut BDA. Stadt=
baurat a. D. Berlin**

**Bild 9: BAUBLOCK DER GEHAG=SIEDLUNG
BERLIN=BRITZ. Architekt Bruno Taut BDA. Stadt=
baurat a. D. Berlin**

Palazzo Farnese, Rome.

Plates 9 and 10 from the margins of p. 163 of the special
issue entitled "Das flache Dach" of the journal *Das neue
Frankfurt*, No. 7, 1927.

Max Ernst Haefeli, Waterwork Houses in Zurich, 1929.

Georg Steinmetz, "Pitched Roofs, Basic Forms"
(Plates. 111–114) and "Porches" in: *Grundlagen für das
Bauen in Stadt und Land, Vol. 1: Körper und Raum,*
Munich 1928.

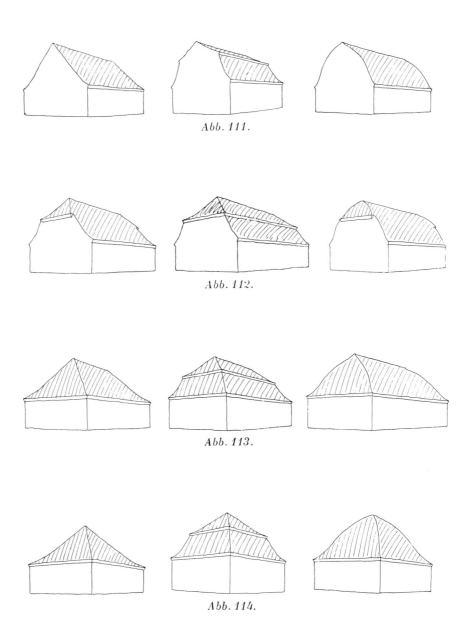

Abb. 111.

Abb. 112.

Abb. 113.

Abb. 114.

*Grundformen: Giebel, Krüppelwalm, Walm- und Zeltdach mit gerader,
geknickter oder gebogener Dachfläche.*

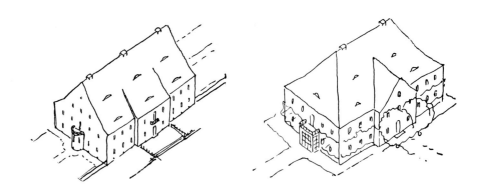

sheltered beneath them are customarily pierced by all sorts of openings or are even formed as open structures. This encourages a reading of a roof as a prism. Our eyes tend to complete their often concealed underside in our imaginations, particularly if it is supported by architectural elements such as a flank front in a closed triangular form or a closed eaves. The roof is then, together with its construction, comprehended as a closed volume, which as a whole bears on the substructure. Even more frequently, roofs appear to be vessel-like hollow volumes which we are accustomed to see as volumes, as the name implies, as soon as their spatially configured surfaces are understood from the outside to be compact, convex forms.

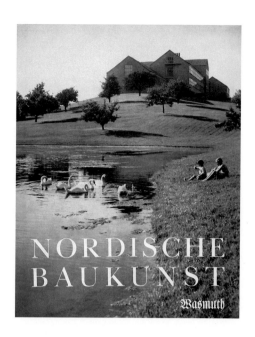

There is an enormous architectural expressive potential in terms of the figurative quality, which roofs can achieve. For example, a sharply down-turned eaves emphasizes the introverted, closed qualities of a house, whereas a centralized hipped roof emphasizes its autonomy. And a flank front signals an openness to the exterior. These formal elements belong to the most familiar and at the same time, the most effective within traditional architecture. Our tendency to see the figure of a roof, or the figure of a house as determined by the roof, in analogy to accustomed bodily forms – and even more so, as dynamic figures – opens numerous possibilities: to give buildings a "face," a "hairstyle," a particular posture or an explicit character, to orient them, to intervene in a space or to retreat from it, etc.

The possibilities of a volumetric architecture[14] can, in the process, be effectively associated with the advantages that are woven into the idea of a roofed house. There is more. It is not without reason that Steen Eiler Rasmussen in his book *Nordische Baukunst* asserts that if it were possible "to retain the roof as an uninter-rupted surface without dormer or window," then one might permit oneself "all possible irregularities […] beneath the roof of such a house […] without invoking agitation, since the mass, the clump, is held together by the roof."[15]

Houses without Roofs

Rasmussen showed how one can accentuate the effect of the "clump" by eliding roof and wall, particularly by means of the use of the same material and the abbreviation of projecting roofs. In an extreme case, which he himself certainly would have rejected explicitly, this creates a volume that is bounded the same way on all sides. We can still see it as house with a roof as long as its form is appropriate, even if, strictly seen, the roof is no longer defined. In this way, for example, we still see the objects made by the artist Katharina Bürgin as houses although they are cast monolithically and homogeneously from paper. It is possible that this occurs because we are conditioned to read the characteristically formed, prismatic volume as constituted of cubic block and triangular prism, of substructure and roof. In all probability, however, we are simply subject to the iconic potential of the conventional form.

In recent architecture, it is noticeably easy to find such volumetric double readings. It seems as though one wanted to maintain the object-like autonomy of buildings as it was established by Modern architecture while simultaneously not wanting to forego the promise of security associated with the idea of roof and house.[16]

The form of the Rudin house by Herzog & de Meuron, with its steep gable and high chimney, corresponds to the archetype of a house (see p. 25). Because, however, everything seems too thin and too abstract, the building is more likely to evoke a drawing or model that a child might make of a house rather than a house itself. The fact, too, that it seems to float above the ground as if on a flying carpet suspends the intensive relationship to the ground which is typically established by roofs, so that the house seems to be travel-ready as the cubic houses of Modernism did.[17]

In the case of the Schaulager, too – to remain for a moment with Herzog & de Meuron – the theme of "house" is simultaneously affirmed and negated. The small pavilion, sheltered by the enormous concave entry front, seems to be closely akin to the main building by virtue of its location and materiality. Its abstracted but nonetheless extremely suggestive house form leads one to expect a sloped roof in the case of the main building; that roof is, however, withheld from the viewer by virtue of his perspective. The pavilion has an effect that is similar to that of the cornice at the Palazzo Farnese: it brings us to identify the Schaulager as a house, appropriate to its specific sheltering function. At the same time, this image is undermined, particularly by the dematerialized sharp-edged-ness of the building, whose smooth white planes meet the coarse concrete structure without mediation and end abruptly towards the sky, as if the building was constructed with no more than paper-thin surfaces. In a highly virtuosic manner, we are inducted into a cabinet of mirrors full of allusions and illusions, where nothing simply is but rather, everything is *like* something: concrete is like earth or rock, metal sheeting is like concrete, a box is like a house, etc. Even the pavilion is, despite its house form, in fact a passage: not a space which invites abidance but rather, a threshold, an interstice.

Such buildings, which play an ambivalent game between pure prism and house, often have a certain melancholic aura. By quoting the appropriate forms, they bear witness to a longing for the house, but at the same time, by negating its essence, to its utopian character. The house seems at that moment just as indispensable as it is definitively lost and unattainable.

1   The word "prism" is used in this text to designate an architectural work whose expression tends to that of an abstract volume. In the original German text, the word "Baukörper" is used. This word embeds the fact that the work is part of the built environment ("Bau") into its designation as a corporeal, solid volume ("Körper").
2   Leon Battista Alberti, *The 10 Books of Architecture*, Book 1, Chapt. 11, New York 1955, p. 16 (Translation: James Leoni).
3   *Herkunftswörterbuch*, Duden, Vol. 7, Mannheim/Leipzig/Wien/Zürich 1963 (German etymological dictionary).
4   On this subject, see Joseph Rykwert, *On Adam's House in Paradise*, Cambridge 1981 (New York 1972); Joachim Gaus, "Die Urhütte. Über ein Modell in der Baukunst und ein Motiv in der bildenden Kunst", in: *Wallraf-Richartz-Jahrbuch XXXIII*, Cologne 1971, pp. 7–70.
5   Martin Heidegger, "Building Dwelling Thinking", in: *Poetry, Language, Thought*, New York 1971.
6   With regard to the many plays on "beneath the roof" and "in the attic", see chapter "Roof and Ceiling."
7   Wolfgang Sonne, in a lecture at the Dortmunder Architekturtage in 2007, appropriately described the gable as the "little brother of the roof".
8   Adolf Behne/Paul Wettstein, "The Aesthetics of the Flat Roof", in: Anton Kaes/Martin Jay/Edward Diemendberg, *The Weimar Republic Source Book*, Berkeley 1994, p. 449.
9   Henry-Russell Hitchcock/Philip Johnson, *The International Style*, New York 1932, p. 71.
10 Le Corbusier, *Towards a New Architecture*, New York 1986, p. 26.
11 Rudolf Arnheim, *The Dynamics of Architectural Form*, Berkeley 1977, p. 135.
12 Hitchcock/Johnson, *The International Style*, op. cit, p. 42.
13 For this reason, it is possible for Rodolfo Machado and Rodolphe el-Khoury to speak of the "Epidermal monoliths" and Hans Hildebrandt can rightfully translate Le Corbusier's concept "volume" into the German "Baukörper". Rodolfo Machado/Rodolhe el-Khoury, *Monolithic architecture*, München/New York 1995, p. 16; Le Corbusier, *Towards a New Architecture*, op. cit., p. 26.
14 Also see: Martin Steinmann, "Forme forte. En deçà des signes", in: *Faces*, No. 19, 1991, pp. 4–13, as well as in: Martin Steinmann, *Forme forte. Écrits/Schriften 1972–2002*, Basel 2003, pp. 188–207.
15 Steen Eiler Rasmussen, *Nordische Baukunst*, Berlin 1940, p. 57.
16 It is fitting that, even in some "blobs" and "monoliths", one finds at the top explicit "roof spaces" with all the corresponding connotations, although nothing would indicate this from the exterior.
17 "Nowadays, the houses in many places look as though they were travel-ready." Ernst Bloch, *Das Prinzip Hoffnung*, Frankfurt/M. 1959, Vol. 2, p. 858.

Roof and Context

Roof and Context

46

Every building exists in a context to which it cannot help but to relate. The forming of the roof is an effective means to gain control over this relationship and to determine its form deliberately. By means of the roof, buildings can be lent meaningful characters. For example, one can orient them so that their massing intervenes in a decisive manner within a space. Or one can determine their character by demanding a particular hierarchical position for them in their context. In this manner, a building's autonomy or its conditionality can be strengthened. The latter is relevant here. This might mean integration or even sublimation in its context; equally, it might mean creating an accent or even contrast. These are all possibilities, which exist equally within a built or natural environment. Whether, for example, a roof is parallel or perpendicular to a steep slope can determine the way a building creates a relationship to topography. By the same token, the way in which a gable or eaves is determined in a party wall context can express differing attitudes towards the space of the street.

Whereas traditional architecture, because of climatic and constructional preconditions, has often given rise to powerful conventions in the form of roofs, these forms today are often the determinative elements of a cultural landscape. Even the concept of "roofscape," which implies a certain homogeneity in roof form and material within a settlement, evidences this fact. To integrate oneself into this culture of roofs – or to distance oneself from it – represents a powerful architectural means with which to make a political statement. The point at which a manifold of architectures is unavoidable, or perhaps even desirable, for example in the case of neighborhoods comprising single family houses or villas, a certain control over roof form can be an efficient means to lending the whole a recognizable character despite the individualistic qualities of the buildings. It allows for a certain tolerance amongst the constituents and between them and their natural context. By examining selected housing projects from the 20th century, Max Bosshard and Christoph Luchsinger demonstrate in their essay an impressive array of possibilities for deploying roofs effectively in urbanistic terms on both sides of their iconic potential. Whether, and in what way, these strategies can be used as planning instruments in neighborhoods which as a whole cannot be controlled formally, is a worthy field for future study.   Martin Tschanz

Integration in Topography

A building can integrate itself into the topography if its roof imitates motifs of the landscape, or if it deflects to the terrain. If the material of the immediate context is used, then this integration can be raised to the level of camouflage. The hotel in Borgafjäll traces the silhouette of the mountains in the background, and the Chalet Vieux near Col du Pillon crouches, with its low-slung hipped roof, against the gentle curve of the landscape which it simultaneously completes. The roof of the mountain station of the funicular in Innsbruck integrates itself into the steep, rocky terrain by virtue of its incline and color palette.

Roof and Context
Staging Topography

Roofs can increase the effect of topography by setting a counterpoint or, equally, by mimicking the topographic form. The latter is true of the terrace housing in Zurich, the massing of which suggests a massive roof, in fact non-existent, which both holds itself constant and follows the line of the hill in heavy parallelism. The convex form of the lens-like roof of the golf club in Totsuka underlines the conti- nuity of the plane, on the other hand, by means of a countermovement, not unlike the church in Passugg: here, the upwardly sweeping roofs, which agglomerate to a tower, emphasize the line of the slope, which becomes even more clear since both its angle and the referential horizontal and vertical axes occur in the roof form.

Claude Paillard **Terrace Housing, Zurich, 1960**
Kenzo Tange **Golf Club, Totsuka, 1963**
Andres Liesch **Protestant Church, Passugg, 1972**

Roof and Context
Landscape and Settlement

Roof form and orientation are often determinate for a cultural landscape, since they relate settlements in a characteristic manner to topography. Pitched roofs with a gable-face orientation as frequently found in the Alpine region, open the houses to the valley and lend the landscape a friendly visage; the orientation of the slope is made explicit in the process, but the exact contours of the terrain are often underplayed.

Orienting the eaves of pitched or even shed roofs to the slope creates the opposite impression of closure; at the same time, the horizontals correspond like contours to the topography. In Avoriaz, the roofs bind the houses together in a larger form, whose silhouette paraphrases the mountain range in the background.

Roofs can be combined to form a continuous roof-scape by virtue of similar form and materials. In the case of Prahin, a village in Waadt, the related pitch of the houses, organized in concentrations, creates the effect that the settlement's roofscape is silhou-etted against the neighboring cultural landscape. The stone roofs of Ticinese stalls, on the other hand, almost meld with their stoney landscape. Analo-gously, the long thatched roofs of traditional Japa-nese houses in Wachi almost become part of the contextual vegetation of the strip-like agricultural fields. The Barak House is draped in green bird protective netting, as is common in agriculture. The color allows the enclosure to read as camouflage.

House and Settlement

In the angled, chaotic conglomeration of the town Arcegno, it is the ameliorating roofs that make the relationships of different buildings legible. In contrast, the hipped roofs facing the Place Ducale in Charleville emphasize the individual buildings while the continuous eaves height, the surrounding arcade and the regular rhythm of the façades lend the square a unified appearance. The street space in a Japanese village in the region of Chubu is defined by two rows of houses whose eaves are oriented to the street. They form the frontage of low-rise commercial buildings, which connect to them at a right angle, then stretch into the existing landscape. This hierarchical structure of communal and individual space is underlined by the roof forms.

Forming Space

The space between buildings can be given different characters by virtue of the roofs. In general, a street or square will be strengthened by buildings whose eaves front them, while a gable-face orientation emphasizes individual houses. Hipped or pyramid roofs, etc., with eaves on all sides in turn emphasize the autonomy of individual volumes. The roof areas of the Bergmann housing project in Hermsdorf create a continuous space, which extends towards the sky. It is modulated and lent ambiguity by the curved street and slope. In the streets of Potsdam's Dutch Quarter, the street space is created by the repetition of adjoining façades, although the houses are clearly recognizable as independent by virtue of their gables. In the case of the Johannishof housing project in Aschersleben, the pyramidal roofs support the character of a constellation among the buildings in a space that remains open.

Ernst Pietrusky **Bergmann Housing Project, Hermsdorf, ca. 1920**
Street in the Dutch Quarter, Potsdam, ca. 1740
Hans Heckner **Johannishof Housing Project, Aschersleben, 1928**

Scale is a decisive parameter for the integration of a building into its context. The subdivision of a roof allows for a large building to be tailored to a smaller-scale context. The powerful volume which comprises the pilgrimage church in Neviges creates a dialogue with the neighboring traditional gabled roof houses by virtue of its serrated, subdivided roof-scape. Because of the homogeneity and particularity of its material, however, the building still reads as an independent entity. The Steigenberger hotel in Saanen refers to the Chalet type. The slippage among the individual roofs produces the effect of a group of single buildings.

The sloped roof can assert itself across several buildings through the continuity of its form, and thus bind these buildings into a single figure. The multi-serrated roof surface of the Ypenberg housing project unfolds across all the buildings and strengthens the unitary reading of the complex. This effect is further supported by the buildings' proportional similarity and homogeneous materiality. In the case of the Kiruna housing project, it was possible to create a relationship between the long, flat buildings in the foreground and the higher buildings in the background by means of a sloped roof that relates to the topography. This also binds the ensemble as a whole.

The Congressional Palast by Libera is characterized by a slightly domed roof which seems to float above the building; it contrasts to the monotone context of EUR. Because the cupped roof recalls a dome, the building is lent a particular significance. While the façade of the University of Coimbra is almost symmetrical, the higher of two roofs indicates the lecture hall which is the most important space. Together with the tower, this roof is visible from afar, making it the icon of the university town.

Roof and Context
Integrating

b & k+ A. Brandlhuber, D. Mandrup   **Crystal Sports Center, Copenhagen, 2006**
Herzog & de Meuron   **Museum Küppersmühle, Duisburg, 1999**

The sloped roof can pick up on different aspects of its context and bind them to one another. In this way, it can act as an intermediary within a heterogeneous context. The sports center in Copenhagen is connected at its ends to preexisting buildings, all of which meld into a unified form. In the museum in Duisburg, the stair tower breaks local symmetry and integrates optically the gable of the middle projection with the cornice of the main building.

A gestural roof can begin a dialogue with its surroundings by means of a suggestive movement. The elegant undulating roof of the main train station's central hall in Rome reiterates the travelers' movement and accompanies them from the train station into the city. The roof of the pub building in Walsall moves with the street's trajectory, then reaches out far into the plaza in front of the building offering views into its interior through the low, glazed front façade. The arced concrete shell which stretches out to form enormous wings, makes the TWA terminal in New York a built allegory of flight. The passengers are literally drawn in under the cantilevered canopy across the entry and into the world of travel.

Eugenio Montuori, et. al. **Stazione Termini, Rome, 1951**
Sergison Bates **Pub, Walsall, 1998**
Eero Saarinen **TWA Terminal, New York, 1962**

The Pitched Roof and the Housing Project

Max Bosshard, Christoph Luchsinger

Thanks to its formal power, the pitched roof develops a manifold of potent meanings in the context of a housing project, even more so than in the case of a singular architectural object. In the addition of similar or differentiated units, which create urban relationships, the roof becomes the primary element within groupings and individuation, within the creation of space, semantic stipulations and cultural references. The pitched roof has of course established itself as the anti-icon of the "Neues Bauen", which for quite some time blocked its use without causing suspicion. Nonetheless, there are numerous examples in the architecture history of the past 150 years – and a concentration of these in more recent times – among which the pitched roof orchestrates the architectural configuration of an urban ensemble.

Individuality and Community

The intention to infuse the artificiality of its form with semantic significance has always been central to the practice of modern housing projects. It was a new home for heterogeneous, mixed groups of individuals and families, for whom industry promised an income as with it, anticipation of a more hopeful future, but who were by no means an organic, socially structured and coherent community. As such, housing was charged with tasks that went far beyond pecuniary demands. The architecture was expected to establish and represent identity, to stage and make apparent social integration.

Among the instruments of socially effective design, in which the pitched roof plays a central role, are neighborly groupings, the indication of central social infrastructure and spaces, a functional typology and the differentiation of primarily public or private exterior spaces. The possibility of identifying housing by virtue of a roof form, and of emphasizing its relative autonomy through formal means, ensured the identity of the single unit. At the same time, the pitched roof served as a binding element among all units in the form of a differentiated row, an articulated repetition, a space-configuring grouping or a modular large-scale form. This is done in exemplary fashion in the Gartenstadt Staaken by Paul Schmitthenner

(Berlin, 1914–1917), in which the many aligned houses are unified in a differentiated manner by hipped or gambrel roofs, while certain elements are picked out by an expressive treatment of the gable.

It is not by chance that the "plurality of the community" often – as is more than obvious in the case of Staaken – makes reference to historically significant precedents, particularly the form of the medieval city with its compact, closely spaced craftsmen's houses, or the village-like vernacular architecture of various provenience which can bring with it an entirely sentimental content. Such very different examples as the Sunnige Hof project by Karl Kündig (Zurich-Schwamendingen, 1943), the Quartiere Tiburtino by Mario Ridolfi, Ludovico Quaroni, Carlo Aymonino, et al. (Rome, 1950–1954) and the Seldwyla project by Rolf Keller (Zumikon near Zurich, 1975–1978) all work with a generalized image of the organic community, and reconcile rural backgrounds with urban reality. In each case, the pitched roof is a binding sign of security and authentic unity.

Beneath the stern gaze of modern theoreticians, such nostalgia-tinged housing could not sustain itself because it undermined the commandment of sobriety; from a postmodern point of view, on the other hand, it could be understood as an effort to find critical proximity to popular culture and thus allow for a much more differentiated evaluation. Staaken, for example, reverts without resistance to the referentiality of bygone small town atmosphere and the unrelenting morality associated with it. Sunnige Hof is extremely agile in its individualistic, petty bourgeois village-like character, whereas Seldwyla still strives for the authenticity of its Mediterranean precedents. Tiburtino, on the other hand, seems like a semiotic laboratory in which the insignia of rural status is confronted with the force of mass housing. The gable roofs set upon eight story high, three unit wide buildings demonstrate the conflict between the scales of rural and industrial housing culture clearly: the figure of the pitched roof withdraws from the prismatic quality of the volume as the number of storeys increases, so that the image dissolves.

Paul Schmitthenner, Garden City Staaken,
Berlin, 1914–1917.

Karl Kündig, Sunnige Hof Housing Project,
Riedacker and Moosacker Colonies,
Zurich-Schwamendingen, 1943.

Mario Ridolfi, Ludovico Quaroni et al.,
Quartiere Tiburtino, Rome, 1950–1954.

Rolf Keller et al., Seldwyla Housing Project,
Zumikon, 1975–1978.

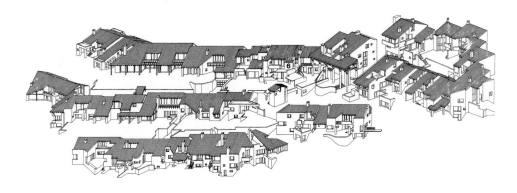

Aldo Rossi, Student Housing in Chieti, Project, 1976.

Michel de Klerk, Sketch of the Workers' Housing Project
De Dagenraad in Amsterdam (1918 – 1923, with Pieter
Kramer).

Zurich Department of Building (F. W. Fissler), Riedtli Housing
Project, Zurich, 1912.

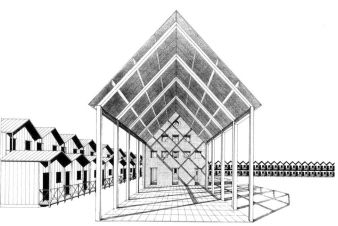

Pitched roof as "pure" sign

Beyond this kind of instrumental semantics, the works of Aldo Rossi refer to the archaic quality of the pitched roof as symbol of rural building, and to an association with the "everyday" architecture of the small Lombard city *(centri minori)*. The difference between, for example, Staaken or Tiburtino and Rossi's elemental use of forms rests upon the fact that the pitched roof in Rossi's architectural language is distilled to an absolute sign which does not pick up on historically determined references but rather only on fundamental architectural configurations. The linking of pitched roofs – with gables oriented to the street – in the project for student housing in Chieti (unbuilt project, 1976), for example, could as easily refer to beach structures, towns in the upper Ticinese valleys or northern German craftsmen's houses. It is, however, precisely by virtue of its indeterminacy that a timeless typological component, which lies behind the form, is uncovered. In Rossi's case, the pitched roof reappears in all possible dimensions and uses, as a tiled roof for row houses, as a glazed roof for conference rooms, as a metal roof for school buildings or columbaria, as a portico, bridge or monument. Rossi's pitched roofs contain space in the sense of a housing, of a collective space, of a shelter, and at the same time, they become completely abstract forms. The element of a prism, triangular in section, reduces the meaning of a pitched roof to an essential geometric form and thus it withdraws itself from any possible pragmatism. It becomes much more of a building block in a stereometric composition. Thanks to all of this, the pitched roof owes Rossi its renaissance as an architecturally valuable solution, after years of polemic exile; at the same time, it is Rossi who "dematerialized" the pitched roof, less so in his built work than in his colorful and theoretical sketches.

Suppressing the Serial

Rossi's polemic was aimed precisely at a purely functionalist interpretation of form, and it allowed him to reference expressionist Modernism. Whereas the "Neues Bauen" located value in seriality, repetition and mass production in terms of aesthetic expression, the pitched roof was used in some modernist projects in order to break seriality or to emphasize the individual element or elements and to repress repetition. The sculptural effect of the pitched roof made closed, "pronounced" forms possible. Piet Kramers and Michel de Klerk's buildings in Amsterdam South (1918–1923) work their way through the entire repertoire of such forms, for example, by drawing out the element of a single house from the overall form through its sculptural qualities. In other cases, it is the subdivision of storeys and different phases of building, or above all the transition from façade to roof that is repressed by pitched roofscapes. The aleatoric tendency of these manipulations is justified by the increased quality of the urban space which is accentuated by the individuated façade and lent a charged atmosphere as a space in itself.

In the Riedtli project in Zurich by F. W. Fissler (1912–1919), the spaces are essentially organized by means of the pitched roof, and the individual building blocks of the project submit to an ambiguous, all-encompassing order. Orientation, symmetry and repetition of the street-oriented gable motif meter and accentuate the exterior space. According to one's reading, spatial figures crystallize and then, like an optical illusion, elide with one another. The pitched roof plays the role of a catalyst which sets the different readings in motion and creates their alternating elisions. Unlike Amsterdam South, in the case of the Riedtli project, the use of the pitched roof subdivides and overlaps the open space and geometry of the buildings' massing into individual pieces – but the roof reunites these fragments to form an ensemble. The double role of the pitched roof as compositional element and as semantic dominant is formulated to the extreme in the Riedtli project.

Roofscape as Topography

There is another, quite different tendency among projects which associate the pitched roof with the underlying land forms, or stated more clearly, which see the land form as the basis for a dynamic roofscape and thus interpret the building group as an expression of its base topography. Whether its topography is shallow or steep, extremely dynamic or gently formed, the potential differentiation in height is exploited for lighting, the definition of building form, and above all, the modulation of a spatial layer between subsurface and roofscape above as an essential element of the housing project composition. Justus Dahinden's housing project in Gaggenau (1982–1985) exemplifies this tendency: a building structure on a flat terrain above which is stretched a net-like roofscape. The weft of this net creates a modulated continuum of narrow, high, low and broad exterior spaces to which various functional and social roles are ascribed. This spatial continuum is even more clearly present in the Tuscolano project by Adalberto Libera (1950–1954) in Rome: a courtyard structure beneath minimally sloped roofs, which maintains an ambiguity in its reading, between additive individual elements and a subtractive larger form. There, the roof plane seems to be a free-floating baldachin – a uniquely elegant solution for the elision of single house and collective housing project.

In the project for a noise-attenuated housing project in Glattal by Roland Stutz (2007), the roofs seem to be no longer a continuous film. Laminar protrusions, which are a reaction to the topographic and flight path noise-determined conditions, are distilled into mathematically defined sculptures which permit different stereometric readings beyond semantic principles. The sloped roof – or rather, the oblique plane – is used here to create an architectural value within the demands of noise attenuation: these are roofs with considerable mass, in the form of earth mounds. The project thus becomes a literal part of the landscape, it grows from it and sinks back into it.

New Units

Another approach, which is in terms of design strategy perhaps even more stringent than the topographic approach, operates by using the pitched roof in a way that seems, paradoxically, almost arbitrary at first. It is based upon the combination of a specific number of elements into a unified whole and then focuses on formal definition. Neither adjacencies nor articulation of serial sequence play a role here, even less so semantics. What is decisive is the development of recognizable groupings, which can mediate between different scales by virtue of their intermediate size. Very often, scale is "filed down", or consciously made ambiguous, as a way of integrating the project better in its context and of slipping the units seamlessly into a larger scale. The whole results from a dynamic system comprising differently dimensioned sculptural volumes from which a heterogeneous series can be formed.

This approach is demonstrated in an exemplary manner by the housing project in Allerheiligen near Wildon in the Styria area of Austria, by the architect Hubert Rieß (1992). Located on the edge of a village on dramatic terrain, the complex, which is relatively large and dense compared to its context, integrates itself effortlessly into the picturesque landscape. Up to three single-family house-like apartments each are combined beneath stepped, shifted roof and wall planes with different slopes to form units. At the same time, the massing develops increasing height towards the center of the complex, so that the relatively low "peripheral buildings" can create a transition to the landscape. Rieß's process is one of *bricolage:* roofs and fragments of roofs, functional units, entire apartment elements, verandahs, wall fragments, spaces, etc., are "cobbled" into a multivalent whole. Here, the traditional pattern of aligning apartment units in rows or stacks is dissolved in favor of new groupings, which become independent in their massing and their lay-outs. Even if it were possibly not the architect's intention, the new units approximate the general order and character of traditional regional building in functional terms – agricultural farms with a combination of work and dwelling spaces, multigenerational households – but also in architectural terms, in that the form expresses pragmatically defined needs.

Whereas in the case of Allerheiligen, this process of decomposition is still largely made

Justus Dahinden, Row House Project in Gaggenau, 1985.

Adalberto Libera, Tuscolano Housing Project, Rome, 1954.

Roland Stutz, Noise-attenuated Housing Project in Glattal,
Semester Project Urban Landscape, ZHAW, 2007.

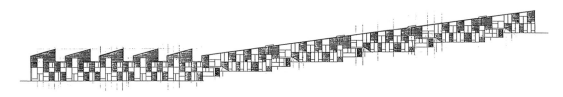

Hubert Riess, Housing Project in Allerheiligen near Wildon,
Steiermark, 1992.

Kaschka Knapkiewicz & Axel Fickert, Competition for
a Housing Project in Wannweid, Wettswil, 1992; model and section.

Bosshard & Luchsinger, Replacement Housing in Schaffhausen,
Competition Project, 2007; elevation.

explicit, inasmuch as the individual components show their isolated form and are only roughly joined, it has again become integrated in the case of the project by Kaschka Knapkiewicz and Axel Fickert for a residential complex in Wettswil (1992) and in our project for a replacement residential building in Schaffhausen (2007). At first glance, the project in Wettswil works with large-scale forms in order to repress seriality and to integrate the forms into the terrain. Upon closer inspection, however, the pitched roof seems to be an instrument which unfolds new creative possibilities for an interlocking of apartments, for the creation of vertical relations between ground and roof, and for the tuning of the spatial sequence within the apartment. Beneath the pitched roof, which corresponds as the formal dominant to the terrain so as to interpret the topography with great agility and sculptural effect, the building blocks of space can be combined in multiple ways without sacrificing any of the massing's power. The design for Schaffhausen may be read in a similar way, although here, it is not the terrain but rather the built context, which determines the matrix for the "housing" of typological manipulation. The combination of differing apartments each with its own circulation and private exterior space – verandahs, gardens, balconies – works to counter the repetition of the housing bars. The pitched roof, nonetheless, slices equal portions from this mass of particles, which are then repeated so as to organize the housing complex at a larger scale. All of this, in the case of Wettswil as well as Schaffhausen, results in a dynamic system of shapes which tend to be freely formable.

Harbingers of Dissolution

In recent times, the geometric matrix of architectural projects has distanced itself more and more from that of the right angle, in which the pitched roof was traditionally almost the only exception. The inflationary deployment of non-orthogonal compositions of walls and roofs has strongly affected the meaning of the pitched roof. It has become, in the meantime, only one amongst many oblique elements in architecture and urbanism, and has lost its role in creating emphasis – De(con)structivism has kept its promise, at least in this case.

It is of course not intended to save the role of the pitched roof over the course of time. But one may still ask oneself about the extent to which such harbingers of dissolution serve the repertoire of design instruments. The fact that the pitched roof can be more than the result of a formal gesture is evidenced by the examples mentioned here. Perhaps it is time to reconsider its role as a constructive architectural element by reconsidering the varied fortunes of the "modern" pitched roof.

Roof as Sign

Roof as Sign

A traditional cultural landscape is almost always characterized by the largely homogenous appearance of its roof forms (see chapter "Roof and Context"). The characteristic roof forms may often be traced back to original construction techniques, particularly to the available roofing materials. Nonetheless, traditional forms often prevail if there is a change in materials. Thus, for example, the steeply pitched forms of straw and thatch roofs were hardly questioned by the "material transposition" to the more durable and predictable material of roof tile. The associated roofscapes transformed, but they did not disappear. Only in the second half of the 19th century did the possibility, or even the demand, arise to choose a roof form and material from an entire palette. The use of traditional forms thus became increasingly an explicit act, even if it was denied. And because the appearance of the roof is so characteristic for traditional building, the roof remains today an extraordinarily powerful sign with which to refer to a particular building tradition, be it the local one into which one wishes to merge, or a foreign or even exotic tradition, which one wishes to evoke in this way.

Seen in this light, it is not surprising that in the 20th century, the flat roof, which at least north of the Alps was only rarely used traditionally, could become a symbol of modernity by virtue of its difference. The question of roofs was well suited to the propounding of cultural politics, whether for or against the flat roof – even if, as Hartmut Frank shows in his essay on the so-called "War of Roofs" in Zehlendorf, this was not necessarily the architects' intention.

Because it is the constitutive element of a house, the roof can be used as a sign to indicate that the fact of "being housed" is the topic of the architecture. And because it is so essential for a house, it is natural to express the particular meaning of a building by virtue of the particular form given to its roof. This is even more true if this uppermost built element has an effect from afar, or if it is raised to lend it that kind of effect.

The essential closed nature of the roof surface and the concomitant tendency to compactness have as a consequence that roofs often have a suggestive form or even seem figural (see chapter "Roof and Prism") – even in the cases in which entire buildings no longer appear as houses but as figures. These are often perceived as built signs or are conceived as such. Roofs in the strict sense of the word are usually no longer recognizable. Martin Tschanz

House as House

The gabled roof has established itself in our culture as an icon for "house". It promises comfort and can be used in architecture if that feeling is to be evoked. The barns of the Po Valley consist only of columns and a simple pitched roof, and the textile tent roof of the emergency shelter in Kobe is provisional. Nonetheless, the roof stands in both cases for shelter and security and makes houses out of buildings. In the rice shop in Tokyo, the familiar element of the tiled roof indicates simple cooking. In the case of the monolithic chapel in Oberrealta, on the other hand, the form of the house is so estranged by means of abstraction that it has been transformed into a sign for "housing" in the broadest possible sense and thus attains a sacral character.

Evocation of a Building Tradition

Roof forms are often characteristic of a certain building tradition and carry its respective meaning. Thus, the roof is an effective means with which to evoke a cultural context. For example, the multiply bent roof of the single-family house in the environs of Zurich refers to the architectural tradition of this rural region. The architectural language of the church in Haparanda, too, refers to vernacular buildings; at the same time, the building interprets the well-known basilica church type. The metal roof on the pavilion in Stockholm with its softly sinuous cornice recalls strange, Far-Eastern architecture and introduces a bit of exotica to the Nordic park complex.

Buildings can function as clearly connoted signs or, given their particular form, be infused with multiple meanings. The store in the shape of a duck which sold roasted ducks became iconic for buildings whose form symbolizes its function. The shell segments of the highway rest stop in Deitingen recall the outstretched wings of a bird, despite their abstraction, and indicate clearly its original owner, the company Mövenpick. Both the opera house in Sydney and the Kunsthaus in Graz, on the other hand, inspire numerous associations. In the case of the former, this has much to do with its location on a harbor, whereas the form of the museum seems to have been appropriated from another world, since it is not associated with its location or its function. The population has embraced both buildings as local landmarks thanks to their extraordinary conciseness.

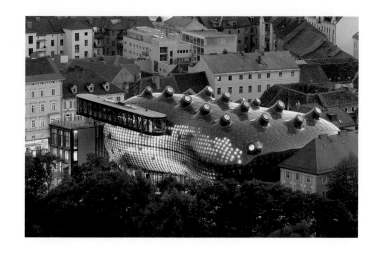

Roof as Sign
Prism and Vessel

The prism and the vessel are archetypal forms in architecture. The asphalt plant in Reichenau recalls a crystal and thus reads as a space-displacing prism. The woven hut in Africa, on the other hand, is a vessel for storing grain and, with its form, embodies the hollow space it contains.

Roof as Sign

Pyramid and Dome

Ieoh Ming Pei **Expansion Grand Louvre, Paris, 1989**
Michelangelo, Giacomo della Porta **Dome of St. Peter's, Rome, 1590**

The pyramid and the dome are cultivated, centralized architectural forms which correspond to the architectural archetypes of prism and vessel. As a glazed prism, the pyramid in the courtyard of the Louvre marks the location of the entrance and the building ensemble's midpoint. Simultaneously, it indicates the underworld of the museum complex. The dome of St. Peter's arches above the holy grave of St. Peter. It demonstrates the singularity of this location as the center of the Catholic Church by dominating its urban environs.

Die hinkende Strasse

Der Dächerkrieg in Zehlendorf

Diese Strasse hinkt —
weil sich in ihr flache und steile Dächer begegnen

Im westlichen Berliner Vorort Zehlendorf ist im letzten Jahre am Rande des Grunewaldes eine neue Siedlung entstanden. In langgestreckten Häuserzeilen und mit sonnigen Hofgärten wurde bei der Anlage dieser neuen Stadt die Naturschönheit ihrer Lage gleichsam in die Wohnstätten hineingeleitet – ein grosser künstlerischer Erfolg der einheitlichen Baugesinnung, zu der sich drei Architekten, Bruno Taut,

Luftbild der Siedlung am Fischtalgrund,
bevor der Dächerkrieg entbrannte. Auf der Wiese rechts vor den Siedlungsbauten ist jetzt die bedauernswerte Sperrkette von neuen Häusern mit steilen Dächern entstanden

Auch dies ist ein Beispiel für die unharmonische Wirkung zweier verschiedenen Bauweisen

liess. In der Steildachsiedlung wurde am 1. September eine Jubiläumsausstellung durch ihre Bauherrin „Gagfah" eröffnet. – Die Muse der Baukunst hat Berlin schon immer stiefmütterlich behandelt. Alle hundert Jahre einmal hat sie einen grossen Baumeister an die Spree entsandt; ihre schönen Bauwerke

Hugo Häring und Otto Salvisberg, bei dieser Schöpfung vereinigt haben. Die Künstler haben am Fischtalgrund das ihnen gestellte Bauprogramm in kubischen Zellen aneinandergereiht und das architektonische Ganze mit flachen Dächern ausgestattet. Und das Flachdach hat hier durch die Einheitlichkeit seiner Durchbildung einen völligen Sieg davon getragen. – Leider wurden die guten Anfänge dieser jungen, schönen Siedlerstadt dadurch zerstört, dass in den letzten Monaten an dem noch frei gebliebenen Strassenrand des Fischtales eine andere Siedlung entstand, deren Häuserkette nicht nur dem Rhythmus der Flachdachsiedlung zuwiderläuft, sondern durch die Wahl des Steildaches als Hausform die frühere Einheitlichkeit des Stadtbildes zerstört hat. Das Fischtal ist dadurch zu einer „hinkenden Strasse" geworden. Es ist sehr bedauerlich, dass im Zeitalter der Wohnungsnot eine gemeinnützige Siedlungstätigkeit so ein verzertes Stadtbild entstehen

Unten: Eine einheitliche Bebauung erzielt immer ein gutes Stadt- und Landschaftsbild

Eine schöne, nicht verschandelte Strasse im Zehlendorfer Fischtalgrund

haben aber an dem Sand der Mark keinen guten Nährboden gefunden. Auch jetzt fehlt der Reichshauptstadt der starke Baumann, der ihr rapides Wachstum mit Weisheit leitet. Siebzehn Architekten haben unter der Führung von Heinrich Tessenow den Zehlendorfer Dächerkrieg entfacht. – Die am gleichen Strassenland feindlich sich gegenüberliegenden Siedlungen werden miteinander nie Frieden schliessen. – Deutschland, und mit ihm die ganze Welt, feiert in wenigen Wochen das traurige Jubiläum der zehnjährigen Wohnungsnot. Der zehnjährigen Jubiläumssiedlung der „Gagfah" wurde diese Not nicht zur Tugend.   G. Stn.

Weltspiegel, illustrustrated weekly extra in *Berliner Tageblatt* from September 9, 1928.

The War of Roofs?
On the Politicization of Architectural Form in 1920s Germany
Hartmut Frank

Did this really happen in Germany, the "War of Roofs"? Architectural histories of Modernism would affirm this, and like to point to roof form as a central criteria for judging either the aesthetic modernity or conventionality of a building as well as the progressive or reactionary mindset of its author or patron. It is in this sense similar to the ribbon window, the corner balcony or even the pilotis. In the historiography of architecture, this war doubtlessly occurred, but it remains an open question whether it also occurred in architecture, at least when we consider the built environment and not only the realm of the thought, spoken or written.

The "Zehlendorf War of Roofs" motivated the German specialized and popular press in 1927 and 1928; given the political developments of the nation during the twelve years of the Thousand Year Reich, it had far-reaching consequences for German architectural discourse well into the 1980s.[1] The cause of this so-called war was the confrontation between two housing projects of different formal layout, particularly with regard to roof form, on the edge of Berlin's Grunewald Forest, in the southern bourgeois district of Zehlendorf. One, the much larger of the two, was built under the aegis of Head of City Planning Martin Wagner with the GEHAG, a housing agency owned by the social-democratic trade unions, according to plans by architects Bruno Taut,[2] Otto Rudolf Salvisberg[3] and Hugo Häring[4] beginning in 1926. The other, smaller project was a housing exposition sponsored by the Gagfah, founded by the German Nationalist Union of Commercial Employees, under the direction of Heinrich Tessenow[5] with projects by a total of sixteen architects, among them Paul Schmitthenner[6], Alexander Klein[7], Paul Mebes[8] and Hans Poelzig[9] to name only a few of those still known today.[10]

Housing as Political Issue

The political background is clear. The Berlin city government, and in particular the ruling Social Democratic party, needed desperately to show success in the area of housing in order to stay true to their election propaganda. The completion of 1915 units in the context of a social housing construction program, sited optimally between a large recreation area and a peaceful bourgeois villa area could not remain undisputed. The election arithmetic and opposing political orientation of the district government promoted conflict, and the press of both political orientations partook greedily. Martin Wagner finally prevailed, and together with Bruno Taut, developed a zoning map based upon the plan already approved by the district in 1924, originally developed by Adolf Sommerfeld, the prior owner of the land, with the Weimar Bauhaus teacher Fred Forbat.[11] Both plans shared a basic structure. Both foresaw about half of the buildings as row houses. The essential difference was the replacement of freestanding single-family houses with multi-storey buildings and thus a significantly higher number of inhabitants.

The program as realized included a similar mix of single-family row houses and three-storey multiple dwellings as in the case of the Hufeisensiedlung, also planned by Wagner and Taut in Berlin-Britz. It was, as such, not exactly workers' housing but rather small-scale housing for the lower middle class, for the swiftly growing new subclass of salaried employees whose favor was courted as much by the Social Democrats as by other parties. There were no individual tenant gardens but rather, a unified landscape plan by Leberecht Migge. Paths were laid to respect terrain and vegetation: the official name "Waldsiedlung Zehlendorf" was programmatic. Later, the name of a nearby restaurant, "Onkel Toms Hütte", prevailed, and was also applied to metro station – built by Alfred Grenander and financed by Adolf Sommerfeld – with a shopping center by Salvisberg. These were not rigidly north-south oriented bar buildings. Instead, a differentiated dialogue between buildings and street space sought to avoid the degradation of unity into monotony by means of protrusions and recessions, the concessions made to vegetation and the bold color scheme. Today, following the exemplary renovation by Helge Pitz and Winfried Brenne, the project is a prized example of Berlin historic preservation. Hardly anyone today can understand why press and parties were able to mobilize one section of the public so effectively against the "bolshevist" form of the project.[12]

With the Gagfah project "Am Fischtalgrund," the local administration and their party compatriots believed that they could offer a fundamentally different housing model: seventy-five flats and forty owner-occupied homes in thirty buildings with 45-degree tiled roofs, all by famous architects. The small project was presented to the public in fall, 1928, in the context of the *Bauen und Wohnen* ("Building and Living") exhibition, and was widely published. If "Onkel Toms Hütte" had at its south end previously only been separated from the green space along the Fischtalgrund by a street, it now received an unwanted neighbor that was, because of its different roof form, immediately understood as a polemic anti-image. Heinrich Tessenow had, with the ostentatious modesty expected of him, planned a long row houses with roof ridges parallel to the street which all followed the same volumetric analysis: a horizontal rectangular prism beneath a triangular prism. All houses had whitewashed or stuccoed masonry, which clearly differentiated itself from the colorfulness of its northern neighbor. Tessenow did not develop a new typology, but instead followed the consequences of a building form which he had already developed in the Garden City Hellerau near Dresden almost twenty years earlier and which had prevailed since then in countless homestead projects throughout Germany. In other locations, the clean modesty of this row of houses would hardly have been noted, but here it produced a conscious contrast, a "limping street," as the newspaper *Berliner Tageblatt* wrote.[13]

The initiators of the exhibition sought this contrast, and its polemic. It did not help that Tessenow had, in the review of *Deutsche Bauhütte,* explained the initial reservations of all the architects involved: "And if we have on one occasion or another, decided to execute the 'Gagfah houses' with normal tiled roofs despite the roofless 'Gehag project', it is not that this decision is rooted in a declaration of war against that project or

its architects, but only in the persuasion that our contemporary housing is not dependent on a certain stylistic direction or modernity, but rather on a definitely simple and reasonable way of building." He mentioned that they all were known to be experienced architects of housing and "some of them closely befriended with […] the colleagues Taut, Häring, Salvisberg […]. It was here and there in its essence a serious search for the best building forms."[14]

Common Ground

There was hardly a critic who noted either the common ground in the aims of both housing projects or the close biographical lineage or numerous similarities in content and work between the architects engaged on each side. At best, there was astonishment at the fact that Häring, Poelzig and Tessenow all belonged to the militantly modernist Berlin "Ring." Everyone stared at the different roof forms. Neither the refined miniaturized apartment plans developed for each project nor the buildings' sobriety and lack of ornament themselves motivated the interest they deserved. Both housing projects represented, above all, this one external appearance, topped out on the one hand flat by roofing paper and on the other, steep by tiles. The roofs were not seen as a requisite element of housing for which, depending on user group, one or the other economic or functional argument was valid, but only as a formal means which could be read and interpreted as a symbol of one's persuasion. For some, a roof belonged atop a house just as a hat belonged on the head of a citizen. For others, the modern metropolitan nomad went bareheaded. His hat had been blown off by the strong wind of modernity and by the same token, he had no need for a roof on his house. It is at the same time noteworthy that in both the northern and southern Zehlendorf housing projects, all houses have complete attics in which occupiable rooms are often placed next to storage areas. The flat, roofing-paper-covered roof was, in this case, certainly a more economical solution than the tiled pitched roof with its romantic dormers, but it was not the desired ingredient of a

The street Am Fischtal, Berlin-Zehlendorf, on the left
the Gagfah housing project and on the right, the GEHAG
housing project, 1928.

Model of the Gagfag housing project "Am Fischtalgrund",
Berlin-Zehlendorf.

M. Wagner, B. Taut, O. R. Salvisberg, H. Häring, Waldsiedlung Zehlendorf alias housing project "Onkel-Toms-Hütte",
1925–1927; to its adjacent southern edge, the Gagfah-
Siedlung "Am Fischtalgrund" (H. Tessenow et al.), 1928.

Großsiedlung Onkel-Toms-Hütte, Siedlung Fischtalgrund

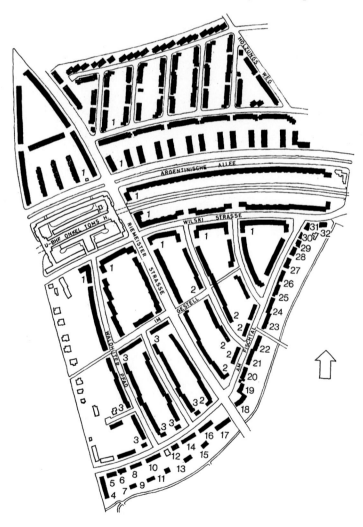

193.1	Bruno Taut
193.2	Hugo Häring
193.3	Otto Rudolf Salvisberg
193.4	Alexander Klein
5	Alexander Klein
6	Alexander Klein
7	Hans Gerlach
8	Gagfah, Entwurfsabteilg.
9	P. Mebes, P. Emmerich
10	Hans Gerlach
11	Hans Poelzig
193.12	Hans Poelzig
13	Hans Steinmetz
14	Emil Rüster
15	Paul Schmitthenner
16	Heinrich Tessenow
193.17	Heinrich Tessenow
18	P. Mebes, P. Emmerich
19	P. Mebes, P. Emmerich
20	Wilhelm Jost
21	Ernst Grabbe
22	Gustav Wolf
23	Fritz Keller
24	Fritz Schopohl
25	Wilhelm Jost
26	Emil Rüster
27	Karl Weishaupt
28	Georg Steinmetz
193.29	Paul Schmitthenner
30	Heinrich Tessenow
31	Heinrich Tessenow
32	Arnold Knoblauch

Walter Gropius and László Moholy-Nagy, buildings for the Gagfah exhibition *Bauen und Wohnen*, "Am Fischtalgrund", Berlin-Zehlendorf, autumn 1928.

On the Problem of the Attic, from Hans Joseph Zechlin's critique of both projects, GEHAG and Gagfah in *Wasmuths Monastsheften für Baukunst*, 1928, p. 549-558, here: p. 552.

Heinrich Tessenow, House 14 in the housing project "Am Fischtalgrund", Berlin-Zehlendorf, 1928.

Heinrich Tessenow, Design for rowhouses for the Garden City Hellerau near Dresden, 1909.

Abb. 8 / Reihenhäuser der „Gehag", gegenüber der „Gagfah"-Siedlung am Fischtalgrund / Der von den unbedingten Anhängern des flachen Daches für überflüssig erklärte Bodenraum erscheint hier als volles Stockwerk und wird durch besondere farbige und plastische Ausbildung zum architektonischen Hauptstück

German single-family house. In the case of inner-city residential blocks, it had forced out the omnipresent pitched roof even prior to the war without debate, as can be seen in the buildings by Taut or Mebes & Emmerich which faced each other among other places in Zehlendorf.

The majority of architects involved really did not make the question of roof form into one of catechism. Taut's later Berlin single-family housing project make unselfconscious use of the classic gabled house typology, and there were only few of the Fischtalgrund architects who eschewed the flat roof in contemporary and later multi-storey housing. The protagonists of the extreme positions who occupy the foreground elsewhere were not involved in the Zehlendorf confrontation, neither Paul Schultze-Naumburg on behalf of the high-pitched roof nor Otto Haesler for the flat one. Walter Gropius was a different story. He had recently been persuaded by Sommerfeld with the prospect of several large commissions to move from Dessau to Berlin and, without many ideological scruples, assumed responsibility for the planning and design of an exhibition pavilion for Sommerfeld's AHAG together with his Bauhaus colleague László Moholy-Nagy on the occasion of the exhibition at the Fischtalgrund.[15] A successful real estate speculator, Sommerfeld thus provided another surprising point of connection between the GEHAG and Gagfah projects. He had provided commuter rail access to both parcels. Both projects were built on his reserve land, his AHAG consortium built the Gagfah houses, and on sites he purchased, architects from both housing projects would later build large projects for both GEHAG and Gagfah in this area of the city, well into the 1930s.

Connections of content among the architects involved run in all directions, although a few complexes are particularly significant. Taut, Salvisberg, Tessenow, Schmitthenner, Mebes and Wolf had all made their name as architects of garden cities in the years immediately preceding the First World War, and all, with the additions of Wagner, Mebes & Emmerich, Knoblauch and Gerlach had all been active in the housing reform move-ment for years. During the war, Häring, Steinmetz, Schopohl, Keller and Wolf had contributed to community projects sponsored by the German Werkbund and by the Deutscher Bund Heimatschutz ("German Heritage Society") for the rebuilding of East Prussia, which had been badly damaged in the first month of the war.[16] Nearly all of them were connected to one another by their collaboration in the German Werkbund, at least until the conflicts surrounding the Weißenhofsiedlung in Stuttgart. Häring, Poelzig, Taut, Tessenow and Wagner were members of the influential Berlin architects' organization "The Ring," to which an oppositional group named "Block" was formed in 1928. Schmitthenner and Steinmetz were among its members, and likely also Rüster and Schopohl.

Divergent Arguments

As early as a half year before the exhibition, Georg Steinmetz published his design for one of his two buildings then under construction at Fischtalgrund. It is one of nearly 1000 examples in a design handbook, which would accompany a generation of German architects in the years to come. On a two-page spread, Steinmetz presents an elongated, simple prismatic building with the obligatory 45-degree roof in full plans and sections, featuring two dormers on each side and articulated by a chimney that punctures the roof on the street side. The building's symmetry is emphasized by a centrally located downspout on the street side and an entry door located in the center of each half of the house's three window axes. On the garden side, there are four window axes respectively and in both of the outermost of these, a protruding, fully glazed, cubic verandah. Despite its very few deviations from the neighboring building, the design follows as an ideal type both Tessenow's precedent and the principle developed in Steinmetz's primer of the simplest solution for every building type. Although it was first published in 1928, this primer was the first of a three-volume work entitled *Grundlagen für das Bauen in Stadt und Land* ("Fundamentals of Building in City and Country"); it was the fruit of many year's scholarly involvement with the rebuilding of East Prussia, with which the Berlin architect had been commissioned in 1915 by a semi-public association for the assistance of East Prussia and by the Deutscher Bund Heimatschutz association.[17] Unlike the previously published documentary second and third volumes, which appeared in 1917 and 1922 respectively, this officially first volume was characterized by a fundamental intention to summarize empirically collected evidence by means of a theoretical, generalized presentation, and to pass it along to German architects once it had been complemented by the additional of countless examples from German and international architectural practice.

This unjustly largely forgotten attempt at a systematic introduction to architectural design followed in principle the dogma already developed in 1913 by the Karlsruhe architect Friedrich Ostendorf, although adapted to the architectural developments of the subsequent fifteen years. Because of Ostendorf death during the war in 1915, he was only able to publish the first volume of a planned six-volume work, *Sechs Bücher vom Bauen* ("Six Books on Architecture"). Drawing from his personal archives, his students and colleagues published two more volumes, but the entire work remains a fragment.[18] Steinmetz, like Ostendorf, avoided any non-architectural argumentation. There are no arguments, which refer to local heritage or national style. He was not afraid to reference the anti-Christ of German traditional Modernism, Le Corbusier, in positive terms.[19] His argumentation begins with the stereometry of the built environment, based upon simple geometric figures, before turning to the principles of spatial definition in the second part and, in the third, examines the geometry of the exterior surface. He pays particular attention to the question of the roof form in a chapter on the volumetric development of architecture.[20] The roof is significant not because the Swabian, Saxon or Bavarian farmhouse have wide roofs, but only because it has the capacity to determine to a great extent the different effects of architecture by virtue of its particular form. Neither the steeply pitched nor the flat roof is *per se* the more appropriate, but each is appropriate in its own way for different applications.

Georg Steinmetz's argumentation is diametrically opposed to that of Paul Schultze-Naumburg's new edition of his *Kulturarbeiten* ("Cultural Works"). This ten-volume work has been extraordinarily productive, for the German reform movement at the turn of the century. The third volume of the revised edition was entitled *Das Gesicht des deutschen Hauses* ("The Face of the German House").[21] This new edition cannot underplay the influence of his cooperation with the theoretician of race, Hans Günther, which was already apparent in his 1928 book *Kunst und Rasse* ("Art and Race"),[22] the book that would form the basis after 1933 for the infamous exhibition *Entartete Kunst* ("Degenerate Art").

For Schulze-Naumburg, there was no critical consideration. He knew what Nordic art was, and he therefore also knew what was German architecture, and what was not. A flat roof was in any case "un-German." The face of the German house was, for him, a product of the German race and it could obviously be read directly in the vernacular architecture of the countryside. Since the mid 19th century, it had been increasingly debased and for German architects, it was now a matter of recognizing its physiognomic traces and expressing them again with force in contemporary architecture. On page 139, we find the image of Bruno Taut's housing bars from the "Onkel Tom" project. They are not particularly commented but rather, because of their flat roofs, dismissed wholesale with other negative examples as "debased." He finds positive examples, on the other hand, in buildings by Schmitthenner, Bonatz, Stoffregen and other members of the "Block," but surprisingly, there is not a single building from the Fischtalgrund housing project. It is not surprising that the ideological turn in the discussion favored by Schultze-Naumburg has diminished the influence of the "Block" and has caused all those advocates of a traditional modernity to stay away if they did not want to or could not share his racism.[23]

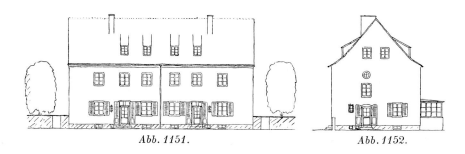

Abb. 1151.   Abb. 1152.

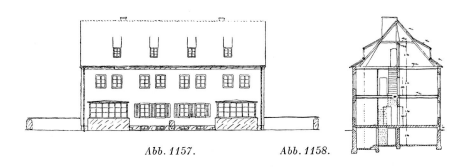

Abb. 1157.   Abb. 1158.

Abwandlungen durch die Dachform.

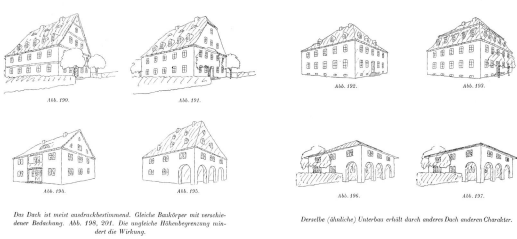

Abb. 190.   Abb. 191.   Abb. 192.   Abb. 193.

Abb. 194.   Abb. 195.   Abb. 196.   Abb. 197.

Das Dach ist meist ausdruckbestimmend. Gleiche Baukörper mit verschie-
dener Bedachung. Abb. 198, 201. Die ungleiche Höhenbegrenzung min-
dert die Wirkung.

Derselbe (ähnliche) Unterbau erhält durch anderes Dach anderen Charakter.

Abb. 198*   Abb. 199   Abb. 200.   Abb. 201.

Georg Steinmetz, House 10 in the Gagfah housing project
"Am Fischtalgrund", Berlin-Zehlendorf, 1928.

Georg Steinmetz, "Roof Forms", 1928, double page
spread in his book *Grundlagen für das Bauen in Stadt
und Land, Vol. 1: Körper und Raum*, Munich 1928.

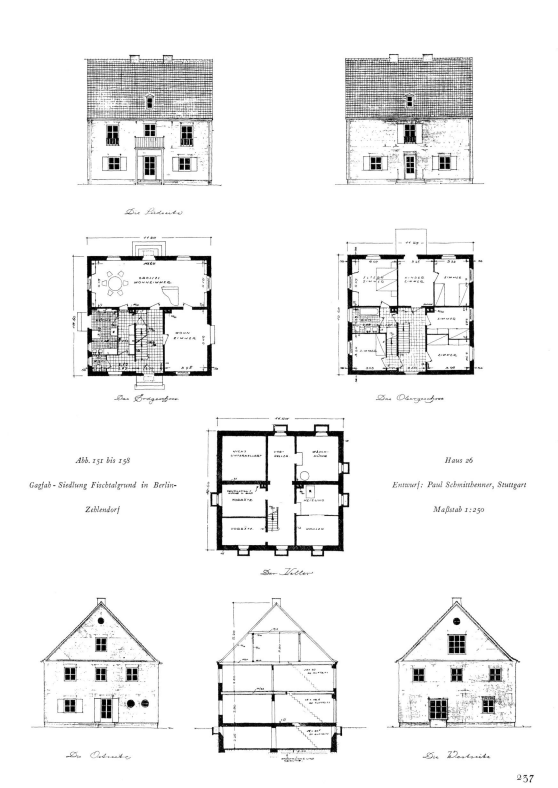

Paul Schmitthenner, House 26 in the Gagfah housing
project "Am Fischtalgrund", Berlin-Zehlendorf, 1928.

Paul Schmitthenner, "The Typology of the German House",
in: *Baugestaltung – Das Deutsche Wohnhaus,* Stuttgart 1932.

Paul Schmitthenner sought a middle position between Steinmetz and Schultze-Naumburg in his 1932 publication with the somewhat unwieldy title *Baugestaltung. Erste
Folge: Das deutsche Wohnhaus* ("Building
Form. First Volume: The German Home").[24]
He begins almost as did his admirer Schultze-
Naumburg by evoking the German people
and the rootedness of German architecture
in German soil, but he leaves this level
quickly to present confidently his own residential buildings as exemplary for the modern type of German house. His historical
precedents are not the regional farmhouse
typology but in essence, a continuous reinterpretation and adaptation of Goethe's garden house in Weimar, in a sense, the house
of the German poet *par execellence* as the
spiritual principle of German architecture.
We know that, for years, he had made this
house type the basis for his instruction at
the TH Stuttgart, the home of the movement, which Werner Hegemann called the
"Stuttgart School" of traditional Modernism.
In his 1932 book, we can once more find the
principles of this pedagogy.[25]

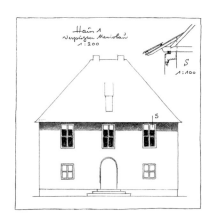

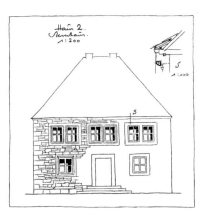

The proximity of his argumentation to
Ostendorf and Steinmetz should surprise us
less if we consider that Schmitthenner, like
Ostendorf, always made reference to his
Karlsruhe studies with Carl Schäfer. This
experience left its clear marks in both theory and pedagogy. In addition, Schmitthenner
had both Ostendorf's and Steinmetz's books
on hand in his bookshelves. For our considerations here, that is of less interest than
his statements about the role and meaning
of the roof, to which he dedicates the chapter entitled "Vom Dach" ("On the Roof"),
in which he writes, "The simple and concise
plan generates the clearest roof form, and
the open plan can only give rise to a good
roof if the individual elements of such a
plan relate to a clear built structure. Do not
believe that you are retrograde if you give
a house a reasonable roof [...] but do not be
an fundamental opponent of the flat roof
under all conditions, but rather, use it with
decorum where it is well and good in its
place."[26]

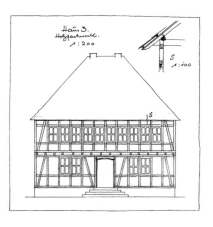

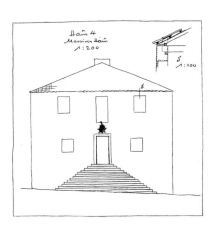

The politicization and ideological polemic
of the discussion around the typology of

the modern house and the form of its roof did not do well to German architecture. The reaction against the blood-and-soil arguments after 1945 and the eulogies to the progressive flat roof along with other stylizations of the "Neues Bauen" movement have not improved the situation. In fact, there was no war of roofs in Zehlendorf but the malign confrontations that ensued in the following Nazi era and, perhaps more influentially, in the democratic post-war period, are not unlike war propaganda. In Zehlendorf, the appropriateness of different architectural solutions for comparable building problems was hardly questioned by any of the architects involved, but the ensuing mobilization of architectural questions for political confrontations was already well developed in its kernel.

1 An almost complete documentation of the "Zehlendorf War of Roofs" can be found in: Christine Mengin, *Guerre du toit & modernité architecturale. Loger l'employé sous la république de Weimar,* Paris 2007.

2 Franziska Bollerey / Kristiana Hartmann, "Bruno Taut. Vom phantastischen Ästheten zum ästhetischen Sozial(ideal)isten", in: Akademie der Künste (ed.), *Bruno Taut. 1880 – 1938,* Berlin 1980, pp. 70 – 80.

3 Martin Steinmann / Claude Lichtenstein, *O. R. Salvisberg. Die andere Moderne,* Zurich 1995 (2nd revised edition), pp. 50 f.

4 Matthias Schirren, *Hugo Häring. Architekt des Neuen Bauens,* Ostfildern-Ruit 2001, p. 164 – 166.

5 Marco De Michelis, *Heinrich Tessenow. 1876 – 1950. Das architektonische Gesamtwerk,* Stuttgart 1991, pp. 293 – 296.

6 Wolfgang Voigt / Hartmut Frank, *Paul Schmitthenner. 1884 – 1972,* Tübingen 2003.

7 Alexander Klein, *Das Einfamilienhaus. Südtyp* (Vol. 1), Stuttgart 1934. (Klein's multiple family dwelling at Fischtalgrund was intended for inclusion in a later volume, which was not published because of his forced emigration.)

8 Paul Mebes, *Um 1800. Architektur und Handwerk im letzten Jahrhundert ihrer traditionellen Entwicklung,* 2 volumes, Munich 1908; and: Edina Meyer, *Paul Mebes. Mietshausbau in Berlin 1906 – 1938,* Berlin 1972. (The Fischgrundtal project only appears in the list of works; it is not commented or illustrated.)

9 Wolfgang Pehnt / Matthias Schirren (Eds.), *Hans Poelzig. Architekt Lehrer Künstler,* Munich 2007.

10 In addition to the architects mentioned, the following architects also realized buildings at the Gefag project: Hans Gerlach, Georg Steinmetz, Emil Rüster, Wilhelm Jost, Ernst Grabbe, Gustav Wolf, Fritz Keller, Fritz Schopohl, Karl Weishaupt, Arnold Knoblauch, Erich Richter, and a team of Gefag architects. "Ausstellung Bauen und Wohnen. Gagfah-Siedlung Fischtalgrund in Berlin-Zehlendorf", in: *Wasmuths Monatshefte für Baukunst,* No. 17, 1928, pp. 211 – 242

11 Annemarie Jaeggi, "Waldsiedlung 'Onkel Toms-Hütte'", in: Norbert Huse (Ed.), *Siedlungen der zwanziger Jahre – heute. Vier Berliner Großsiedlungen 1924 – 1984.* Berlin 1984, pp. 137 – 158

12 Steinmann / Lichtenstein, *O. R. Salvisberg. Die andere Moderne,* op. cit.

13 *Berliner Tageblatt,* 9. 9. 1928, quoted in Mengin, *Guerre du toit & modernité architecturale. Loger l'employé sous la république de Weimar,* op. cit., p. 61

14 In: Heinrich Tessenow, "Der Zehlendorfer Dächerkrieg. Die dachlose 'Gehag', die bedachte 'Gagfah'", in: *Deutsche Bauhütte,* No. 14, 1928, p. 213.

15 See Winfried Nerdinger, *Walter Gropius,* Berlin 1985, pp. 108 and 246.

16 Hartmut Frank, "Heimatschutz und typologisches Entwerfen. Modernisierung und Tradition beim Wiederaufbau von Ostpreußen 1915 – 1927", in: Vittorio Magnago Lampugnani / Romana Schneider (eds.), *Moderne Architektur in Deutschland 1900 bis 1950. Reform und Tradition,* Frankfurt a. M./ Stuttgart 1992.

17 Georg Steinmetz, *Grundlagen für das Bauen in Stadt und Land mit besonderer Rücksicht auf den Wiederaufbau in Ostpreußen,* Vol. 2: "Besondere Beispiele", Munich 1917; Vol. 3: "praktische Anwendung", Munich 1922; Vol. 1: "Körper und Raum", Munich 1928. (His semi-attached house in Fischtalgrund in Vol. 1, pp. 316 – 318.)

18 Friedrich Ostendorf, *Theorie des architektonischen Entwerfens,* Vol. 1: "Einführung" (= Vol. 1 *Sechs Bücher vom Bauen*), Berlin 1913.; *Sechs Bücher vom Bauen,* Vol. 2: "Die äußere Erscheinung der einräumigen Bau-

ten", Berlin 1914; Sechs Bücher vom Bauen, Vol. 3: "Die äußere Erscheinung der mehrräumigen Bauten", Berlin 1920.

19 Steinmetz, *Grundlagen für das Bauen in Stadt und Land mit besonderer Rücksicht auf den Wiederaufbau in Ostpreußen,* Vol. 1, op. cit.; on Maison Citrohan: "Mediterranean dwelling. The clear, simple organism of the house is oriented towards the pretty view." In opposition, on p. 385, the two houses at the Stuttgart Werkbund exhibition of 1927 are accused of grotesque deformity.

20 Ibid., pp. 396 – 418.

21 Paul Schultze-Naumburg, *Das Gesicht des deutschen Hauses. Kulturarbeiten* (New edition), Vol. IV, Munich 1929.

22 Paul Schultze-Naumburg, *Kunst und Rasse,* Munich 1928.

23 For example, Werner Hegemann and Fritz Schumacher begin quickly to distance themselves from the "Block" and its increasing affinity for the NSDAP.

24 Paul Schmitthenner, *Baugestaltung. Erste Folge: Das deutsche Wohnhaus,* Stuttgart 1932.

25 Werner Hegemann, "Die Architektur der Architektur-Schule Stuttgart", in: *Wasmuths Monatshefte für Baukunst,* No. 33, 1928, p. 473 (more on the Stuttgart pedagogy, pp. 474 – 520).

26 Schmitthenner, *Baugestaltung. Erste Folge: Das deutsche Wohnhaus,* op. cit., pp. 22 ff.

Roof and Aperture

Roof and Aperture

With the reuse of attic spaces, the demands placed on light, view and exterior space are transformed, which often creates a need for more apertures. To fulfill this demand nonetheless proves difficult. While an aperture can of course be a natural component in the architectural construct of a wall, roofs want to appear as complete and compact as possible since the role of protection is part of their essence. Marc Loeliger writes, "[t]he introduction of apertures bring light into the attic will always raise the issue of the roof's integrity. It is only possible to avoid creating an aperture that seems to be a malignant caesura in the roof's surface if it becomes an integral part of the roof volume."

But when is an aperture an integral part of a roof? This seems to depend upon the relationship between the single aperture and the roof volume as a whole. Thus, for example, many perforations may together form a pattern. In the process, the single penetration loses significance and becomes part of a whole; this can, moreover, refer to the roof's unified form and strengthen it. In case of structural openings such as gaps between roof planes, the individual components remain unharmed, and the geometry of the roof undisturbed. This is also true if entire component surfaces of a roof become porous, going as far as a glazed roof, in which case it is impossible to speak of an "aperture". It is not a coincidence that one might speak of a roof skin: we are most likely to understand an aperture as a wound if we are given the impression that a piece of the roof is missing because it has been removed. Such wounds disturb the integrity of the roof greatly and are therefore only possible as an exception. The best building codes try to deal with them, but presume conventional roof forms. Innovative roof solutions are thus in practical terms difficult to realize: there is a paucity of appropriate building code instruments designed for them. The extent to which there is a need for change in this respect can be deduced from the many inspired student projects which evolved in the experimental context of a design courses. As Marc Loeliger describes, they demonstrate some surprising suggestions for apertures in roofs, or better said: for the open roof.

Christa Vogt

Camouflage

The roof plane windows at the Saiko House in Ashiwada are, during the day, hardly visible under a
translucent roof skin, very different from the additive
dormer.

Roof and Aperture

Partial Surface as Aperture

If apertures subsume an entire portion of the roof surface, they can be integrated without disturbing the building volume. The Hindustan-Lever Pavilion in Delhi comprises segmented planes, which were partially entirely open, and the Björnson Studio in Los Angeles can be read either as a cubic prism with chamfered corners or as a building with glazed pitched roof.

Apertures can be integrated wherever the surface of a volumetric roof is extended beyond the edge defined by the building's geometry. The roof of the atelier house in Zumikon, which protrudes beyond the ridge, shelters the windows below it. In the case of the scout hut in Lovön, there are four roofs which shift towards a peak to form an asymmetrical hood above the fifth one. The upper surface of the mansard roof in the Liebrecht House in Hanover is in part extended so that vertical openings can be formed in the steeper portion of the roof. In the row houses in Glarus, it is the façade which is extended upwards to form a gable-like roof tower, thus making of the roof a dynamic silhouette.

Wounds

An aperture is perceived as a wound if it perforates the roof surface in such a way that a portion of the roof skin seems to be missing. Wounds are exceptions, which always exist in a critical relationship to the rule. The various apertures of the Perlbinder House in Sagaponack are cut into the building volume. One aperture intersects the eave and thus, together with the homogeneous materialization, emphasizes the sense that the house is a compact volume. The apertures appear to be part of its relief. The opposite of cuts are additive dormers. As the house in Bergamo demonstrates, they do not interfere with the impression of a roof that runs continuously beneath them. In the case of the Müller House, sculptural cuts are combined with flush apertures. This makes clear that these different kinds of apertures both function as wounds.

Norman Jaffe **Perlbinder House, Sagaponack, 1974**
Giandomenico Belotti **Single-Family House, Ponterancia, 1975**
giuliani.hönger Architekten **Müller House, Unterägeri, 1996**

Straddling

Openings can be formed by the incision and forking of a roof surface. In that case, the degree of injury is much less than is the case when a portion of the roof is missing. The roof plane of the Löwen pharmacy in Thorn arcs repeatedly, like winking eyes, culminating in oval dormers without undermining the sense of its continuity. And between the aligned, oblique shells of the warehouse in Montevideo are yawning openings which give the impression that they could be drawn together again. This is also true for the left-hand of the two houses in Stavanger, although it is severed by a forking gap.

Löwen Pharmacy, Thorn, ca. 1800
Eladio Dieste   Warehouse, Montevideo, 1979
Helen & Hard   Two Houses, Stavanger, 1999

Löwen Pharmacy, Thorn, ca. 1800
Eladio Dieste   **Warehouse, Montevideo, 1979**
Helen & Hard   **Two Houses, Stavanger, 1999**

Single openings can be subsumed in a whole if they are perceived to be part of a pattern. This is the case in the Brussels City Hall, where the entire roof is emphasized by an ornamental pattern of dormers and their perspectival effect. In the Klosterneuburg church there is ambivalence as to whether the roof is penetrated by numerous skylights or whether it is a dimpled roof. The Japanese Pavilion in Hanover has no apertures in the true sense. It consists of an open cage whose grid pattern shines through the translucent paper membrane.

Determining Figure

Apertures are not seen as disturbances in a roof if they are an essential component of the overall figure of a building. Thus, gabled windows and oval dormers create in the case of the Riehl House in Neubabelsberg a kind of determinate symmetry, which the façades and plan do not follow in all details. The over-dimensioned window of the semi-nar building in Järna accentuates the building's middle and simultaneously integrates roof and wall by extending beyond the roof's edge. In the Cantonal Library in Liestal and in the school complex in Zurich, apertures are developed from the ridge of the roof to generate characteristic silhouettes which determine the buildings' forms.

Leandro Costa, House for an Antique Dealer in Steckborn,
Semester project 4th Year, WS 2005/06.

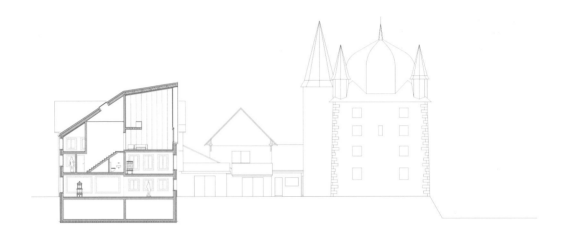

The Sky in View

On the topic of the aperture in the pitched roof at the Center for Constructive Designs at the Zurich University of Applied Sciences in Winterthur[1]

Marc Loeliger

In light of the enormous quantity of folded surfaces, segmented prisms and sculpturally deformed volumes in current architecture publications, it seems that the meaning of the pitched roof is shifting from unsophisticated garret to a rich field of research for ambitious architects. The background of this new state is the increased use of the space beneath the sloped roof as living and work space, which generates new preconditions for this traditional structural element. The demands for warmth and cooling, for light and view, for air and exterior space demand new ways of thinking relative to form and structure, especially relative to the aperture.

Since 2003, the Center for Constructive Design at the Zurich University of Applied Sciences in Winterthur has run a series of design studio courses which considered the question of the pitched roof. The basis for the subsequent examination of the aperture in the pitched roof derived from some of the work completed in the four courses prior to 2006.[2] The problems given vary widely in terms of their scale, their contextual relationships and their program, and thus allow the consideration of this theme in terms of multiple aspects and questions. The experimental laboratory which is inherent to the courses makes it possible to circumvent the often narrowly defined parameters of building codes, costs, functional demands and constructional reality. That does not mean, however, that these important issues are not significant for the coursework. Nonetheless, they are interpreted as a "possible reality" in order to open the space for innovation and new interpretations. The potential of the work shown here is derived not least of all from these freedoms.

The space beneath a sloped roof was always special. Traditionally uninsulated, often with a low ceiling height and only few possibilities to bring in light, it was no more than storage space or accommodation for servants. The renovation of this ancillary space in the single-family suburban home often lead to a transfigured image, something between do it yourself and romantic homeliness. The attempt in these courses was to examine the atmospheric particularities of the attic and its openings, to interpret it in new ways and thus to formulate an architectural counterposition to the clichéd assumptions.

The introduction of apertures to bring light into the attic will always raise the issue of the roof's integrity. It is only possible to avoid creating an aperture that seems to be a malignant caesura in the roof's surface if it becomes an integral part of the roof volume. It is obvious that, despite the enormous spectrum of project briefs offered in the various design studio courses, certain repeated aperture types emerge which best fulfill this requirement.

Blow up

To amplify, alienate or recontextualize the traditional elements of roof lighting and thus to facilitate a new reading of the roof volume is not a new strategy. We find these techniques in the expressive designs of proto-Modernism, in the early years of the 20th century. Some examples are the deliberate, towering roofscapes of Hans Poelzig. They are also found in buildings of the late-modern period, whose protagonists in the 1950s in Italy and Scandinavia sought to test the defining potential of the sloped roof. Different student projects return to this method. There, it is not uncommon to find ironic, facile playfulness in dealing with inherited forms, a way of working that leads to surprisingly new roof images and forms.

Typical of this uninhibited approach is the design by Leandro Costa for an apartment house with an antique shop in the historical context of Steckborn on Lake Constance: on its street side, the volume integrates itself into the historically developed row of houses along Seestrasse. Facing the lake, the primary living space distends the traditional pitched roof from the inside to create a two-storey mega-lucarne. With a punctual shift in scales, the roof forms a new relationship with the neighboring tower courtyard, typical of the town, and stages the significant view to the lake by means of this gesture. This measure makes it possible to bring interior light deep into the volume and to make the presence of the particular roof apparent below the cornice line.

The project by Daniel Blank, built above an existing residential building in the Zurich

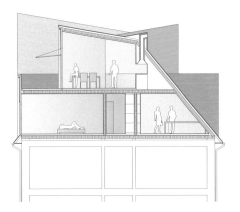

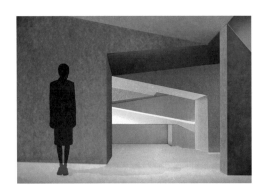

Oberstrass quarter, plays with the perception of traditional rooftop additions by creating an unusual relationship between the two. The entire roof is formed by an alternating series of differently shaped one- and two-storey dormers. The clever alternation of vertical elements and a scalar variation permit the roof to be read as an independent element despite the large part of the vertical surface. Exterior spaces can, in accordance with the system's logic, be positioned as terraces above the dormer. The interspersing of vertical elements recalls a familiar image of grouped chimneys. Thus, the effect of the roof volume shifts unexpectedly between the expected figure of roof and rooftop addition, and a new image of a dynamic roofscape. On the interior, the project indicates an enormous spatial potential by virtue of the fact that spaces can be combined laterally, longitudinally or vertically. In atmospheric terms, the spaces are characterized by the sloped roof surface, but their dimensions are surprising, as are their lightness and the large proportion of apertures with views to the neighboring roofs.

By means of reinterpreting a well-known type, the rooftop addition, the students succeeded in reconsidering the entire roof as building component on a variety of levels. The formulation of rooftop additions determines the form of the prism, interior space, exterior space, light and atmosphere. This creates a new type, which can be interpreted relative to site and integrated into the cityscape; in this sense, it could have the character of a model for the necessary reformulation of building codes for attic renovations.

Peaked Caps

The aperture at the peak of a roof is a typology which can already be found in ancient architecture. At the same time, the puncturing of this delicate area of the roof raises questions regarding more than those of construction and cannot be considered a traditional method for top-lighting in our latitude for non-religious buildings. A considerable number of student projects pursued this strategy. In particular, the museum designs for Munich and Torino frequently

Deana Canonica, Art Museum in Torino
Semester Project 4th Year, WS 2004/05.

Daniel Streuli, House for an Antique Dealer
in Steckborn, Semester Project 4th Year,
WS 2005/06.

have recourse to this form of roof aperture;
in these cases, top-light is given great importance within exhibition spaces. The design
by Deana Canonica is exemplary of this
approach. Its large roof area is subdivided
into individual pitched roofs topped by
lanterns. The sloped roof surfaces are able,
unlike skylights in flat roofs, to transport
light and to distribute it evenly.

But it is also possible to find residential
projects with this type of top-lighting aperture. The design by Daniel Streuli for a
live/work building inhabited by a dealer in
antique tiled ovens at the center of Steckborn at Lake Constance transforms the
entire roof into an enormous light funnel. A
solid wood construction based upon a rigid
grid binds the expressive roof form to the
three-storey, timber load-bearing structure
below. Such elements as chimneys or dormers are transformed and integrated into a
continuous overall form. The apertures here
are not incisions into the roof surface but
rather integral parts of the roof volume
within whose surface private living spaces
are nested. In section, it is possible to see
that the roof not only determines the building's external appearance but also determines the interior space far below the cornice line. The project's surprising moment
is the refined transposition of conventional
expectations regarding the traditional
domestic roof, and the persuasive translation
in the interior space of a romantic idea of
living beneath a sloped roof.

Roger Küng worked on the same site with
an interior space that is simultaneously very
traditional and modern. The central space
(in more than one sense) peaks along the
entire building height and is lit by a hexagonal opening that can be opened in summer.
Like the central space of a Palladian villa,
it is simultaneously interior and exterior
space, and comprises the kernel of the
house's spatial organization. Superimposed
flights of stairs which serve in alternation
the public and private circulation move up
in a spiral form and create an illusionist
effect that changes in spatial terms from station point to station point. The void space,
developed from the idea of the tiled oven, is
the multiply bent and compressed imprint

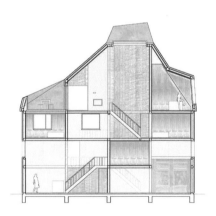

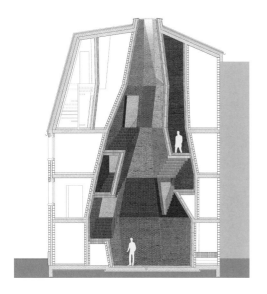

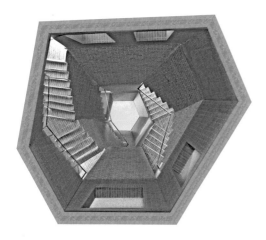

Roger Küng, House for an Antique Dealer in Steckborn, Semester Project 4th Year, WS 2005/06.

of the prism and characterizes the form of the living and work spaces by virtue of its polygonal plan geometry. The house-in-a-house derives its internal suspense from this symbiosis. It is only beneath the roof that the alternating relationship again flips: the hollow space of the light core becomes a sculptural object. It is made relative by a second volume with a stair to the roof, and by the chimney, which hangs from the roof. It is set into a fascinating, multiply broken roof surface, recalling the interior of a kaleidoscope.

Origami

There are many instances in which the subdivision of the entire roof into smaller segments is deployed by the student projects, much like traditional Japanese paper folding. This strategy may have scalar, contextual or geometric reasons: but in every case, the result is a sculptural deformation of the roof which permits great geometric freedom compared to traditional roof forms. By omitting or glazing certain segments, it is possible to integrate apertures without disturbing the roof's overall form.

The project for a rooftop addition to a residential building in Zurich by Andreas Garraux operates with this method. Akin to organic crystals, the uneven roof surfaces sit upon the existing 1940s building. The segments are made of timber elements which behave statically like a folded plate and thus stiffen the roof. Large incised apertures create accents in the volumes and organize the residential units in plan and section. The incisions allow for all window surfaces to be vertical and sheltered from rain, thanks to a refined sectional solution, and thus for all spaces to be provided with daylight of different qualities. They form exterior spaces which face south, deploying the particularities of their location between faceted roof surfaces. On the interior space, this solution leads to multilayered relationships and surprising spatial sequences. The combination of pointed and blunt spatial boundaries allows for the genesis of multiple spatial configurations whose richness of geometry and light qualities is akin to polished crystal. The usual terminology of

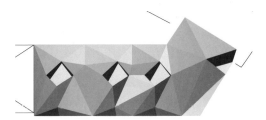

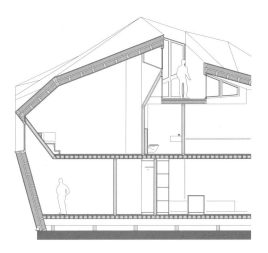

building codes – roof window, rooftop addition, one-third rule – is no longer an adequate measure, creating a demand for the formulation of new categories.

With a Wink

The opening of the juncture between wall and roof is traditionally found in Switzerland in hay barns. The protected juncture beneath a wide-spanning roof is spread apart to provide daylight for the unheated spaces and to allow for ventilation. In contemporary architecture, the corresponding juncture is often used as a means to emphasize the independence among the different building components. This is true in the case of the significant gap between wall and roof in the Ronchamps chapel by Le Corbusier,[3] although it is used less for daylight rather than for the purpose of allowing the roof to appear to float.

The project by Tobias Ziegler for a house of a potter at the center of Steckborn tries to make a formal separation between the wall and roof. The gap in this case is, however, spatial. Facing the view, the masonry wall and the flatly sloped roof diverge, so that a covered exterior space is formed. Like a winking eye below the brim of a hat, the living space looks out beyond the roof and focuses its gaze on the depth of Lake Constance.

In the project for a residential building with gallery in Steckborn's green belt by Michèle Säuberli, there is a dialectic relationship between wall and roof surfaces. Spanning above the wooden prisms, precisely integrated into its site, is a roof comprising triangular segments, which stretches like a tent from corner to corner. The robust construction connects the two different building components. By straddling the joint in the vertical direction, it is possible to offer light and view to the attic spaces behind. At the same time, the gap is also stretched into the horizontal and forms an outdoor space between the exterior and an interior façade, each of which extends downwards to a different level. These act like light courts for the entire building and make a complex internal spatial network possible, which creates relations within the volume

Tobias Ziegler, House for an Antique Dealer
in Steckborn, Semester Project 4th Year,
WS 2005/06.

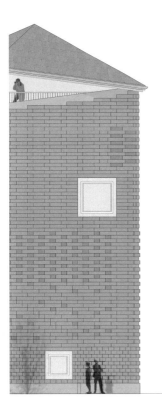

from space to space and storey to storey. The space beneath the tent-like roof has a fascinating ambivalence: on the one hand, the depth of the two-layer façade and the presence of the bearing structure convey a sense of comfort. On the other hand, the roof's quality of a stretched textile exudes a lightness which recalls the ephemeral essence of nomadic tents.

Roof Volume and Urban Space

"A vast part of the earth's surface, in a town, consists of roofs. Couple this with the fact that the total area of a town which can be exposed to sunlight is finite, and you will realize that this is natural, and indeed essential, to make roofs which take advantage of the sun and air," according to Christopher Alexander.[4] Attics contain the most significant space for expansion in the center of our Central European cities. Hidden here is an immense potential for densification, which does not require the occupation of new ground plane space. The possibility of this kind of growth in section demands the input of building departments and historic preservation, but in particular, of architects.

The student projects allow for speculation that the traditional understanding of the roof as an independent building component is more equipped to respond to the demand for a new interpretation of the roofscape as urban space of occupation than is the more common contemporary strategy of the "All-over." Too often, the pitched roof is used as an alibi today for formalistic, sculptural distortions. The roof should be treated as a roof, not as a stretched or bent extension of the façade. This can only be achieved when the traditional meaning of the pitched roof is understood and if the context is the basis for working, if the structural logic is respected and if these conditions are brought together in an atmospherically dense construct, able to house new functions.

As the coursework demonstrates, this does not mean that the effect of the roof must end at the cornice line. On the contrary, many of the projects make an effort to think the roof and façade surfaces together and equally. Similar to the residential and commercial building by Asnago Vender from

Michèle Säuberli, House for an Art Collector in Steckborn,
Semester Project 4th Year, WS 2005/06.

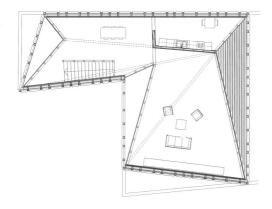

Asnago Vender, Apartment house in Milan, 1961.

Kartin Bürgi, House for an Antique Dealer in Steckborn, Semester Project 4th Year, WS 2005/06.

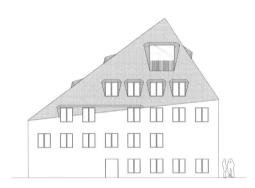

the 1960s on Via Andrea Verga in Milan, the project by Katrin Bürgi in Steckborn blurs the boundary between the two building components through the use of similar windows above and below the cornice line; it does so without undermining the integrity of the roof.

For the interior space as well, measures are taken to extend the atmosphere of the space beneath the roof downwards into the depths of the building. The roofs impact the projects in a reversal of the traditional "from above to below" thinking as the generator of the sectional solution: the world of the attic with its mysterious atmospheric qualities exudes its influence deep into the building volume. In this way, the newly accessed roofscape becomes a formative, palpable part of the newly interpreted urban prism. Just as many cities in the past decades have reintegrated the river and lake banks which had been occupied by industry and the back side of urbanity, today it is the "above" of the city, its nexus to sky and light, which is the urban space capable of reinterpretation and potential improvement.[5]

Here, too, it is not the demand for a way of working oriented towards the spectacular which is at stake. In order to provide these newly acquired spaces with light, air and view, it is inevitable that the roof be opened. This can only be architecturally successful if the roof is taken seriously in its historical significance and contextual relationships; at the same time, success also depends on the ability to transpose traditional images into new forms in response to new demands.

1   Beginning in fall, 2007, at the Zurich University of
    Applied Sciences in Winterthur.
2   Fourth year course, winter semester 2003/04: Sloped
    Roof. Museum of housing in Wald and Maienfeld, studio
    critics: Axel Fickert, René Hochuli; fourth year course,
    winter semester 2004/05: Munich and Torino. Two
    Museums of Art, studio critics: Axel Fickert, René
    Hochuli; fourth year course, winter semester 2005/06:
    Distant Views: Living and Working in Steckborn, studio
    critics: René Hochuli, Marc Loeliger, Astric Staufer;
    master's course, summer semester 2006: Above the
    Roofs. Living in Zurich, studio critics: Astrid Staufer,
    Beat Waeber.
3   Willy Boesiger (ed.), *Le Corbusier – Œuvre Complète,*
    Vol. 6, 1952 – 1957, Zürich 1957, pp. 16 – 41.
4   Christopher Alexander / Sara Ishikawa / Murray Silver-
    stein, *A Pattern Language,* New York 1977, p. 567.
5   Matthias Bräm, *Über den Dächern. Innovation Aufstock-
    ung Steildach,* Evaluation of Projects 1, Masterstudio SS
    2006, Winterthur, ZHAW, 2007, p. 7.

Roof and Ceiling

Roof and Ceiling

At the transition between the chapters concerned with the external appearance of the roof and those which concern themselves with the space beneath it, this chapter examines the relationship between exterior and interior, between roof and ceiling.

On the one hand, the formation of an exterior shell which defines the roof and, on the other, the internal shell which defines space has a long tradition. The architectural potential latent in the conscious configuration of the relationship between roof and ceiling is nonetheless only seldom deployed. Much more often, the often coincidental leftover spaces negotiate between volume and interior space which were designed without any relationship between them. This case is, however, of no interest here. The examples on these pages are intended much more to show the possibilities inherent in relating effectively roof and ceiling. In doing so, there are fundamentally two ends to the spectrum: roof and ceiling create the same or a contrasting effect. In order to maintain control over them, it is important to pay attention to one essential characteristic, which distinguishes the spatial roof and the flat roof. Whereas the exterior appears as a volume, the interior creates a vessel. This is less banal than it seems. Concave and convex forms are perceived entirely differently, even if they are two sides of the same entity. On the other hand, in some cases, roof and ceiling must be differently formed for the appearance of exterior and interior space to correspond respectively.

Since the relationship between "interior and exterior silhouette," as Jacques Lucan formulates it, cannot be comprehended in single pictures, the images relating to this chapter are structured differently than all the others: each project is documented by an interior view, an exterior view and a

section. It is only possible in this way to make the relationship between roof and ceiling transparent.

Jacques Lucan demonstrates, above and beyond this point, that the interstice between interior and exterior must also be considered. He connects this with the poché of the 19th century and, by virtue of this connection, has access to an architectural history that is also a potential for the future. Not only can the subordinate areas contained in poché be reinterpreted as light, storage or mechanical spaces, but they can also represent a value in and of themselves. Thus, although a traditional attic may, for example, usually be generated coincidentally, it offers a dusky, angular, mysterious space that is also the antithesis of the postulates of Modernism[1] – a yet-untapped atmospheric potential.

Barbara Burren

---

1 "[…] it [the flat roof] ends the house at its top exactly where its functions end, without the addition of the unclear, irrational attic with its mysticism." From: Josef Frank, "Akzidentismus", in: Mikael Bergquist/Olof Michélsen (Eds.), *Josef Frank Architektur*, Basel 1995.

Paralleling and Diverging

Roof and ceiling of the Park Theater in Grenchen parallel each other and yet the effect on the interior and exterior is entirely different. While the roof, seen from the exterior, conjoins with the other oblique planes to form a rolling landscape, the ceiling isolates the auditorium by means of a rolling gesture that integrates rear wall and balcony. In the Church am Steinhof, the interior space is understood as the correspondent to the dome although the latter is actually almost twice as high in order to read as a sign at an urban scale.

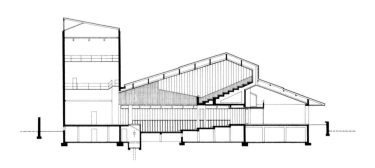

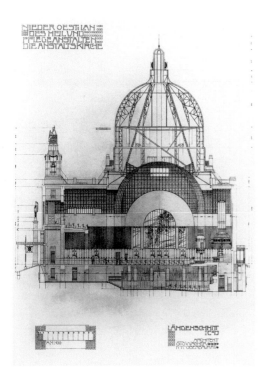

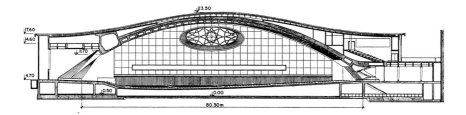

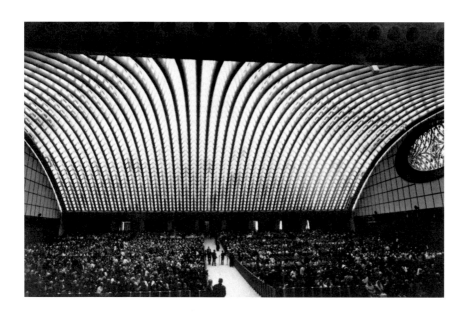

The papal audience hall in Rome and the home for the aged in Alvaneu exploit the phenomenon that a slight difference between ceiling and roof is not noticeable. In both cases, the similarity between interior and exterior is so great, that the building appears to be a unified organism, although interstices (poché) are created which can fulfill other, varying secondary requirements.

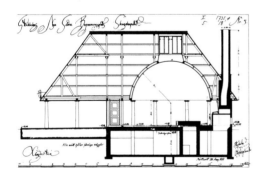

With a contrast between roof and ceiling, the unified effect of a building is fractured and the difference between interior and volume becomes central. While the drawn-down hipped roof of the small chapel in the woodland cemetery in Stockholm evokes a forest hut when seen from outside, the top-lit dome on the inte-

rior creates a sacred atmosphere. In the case of the Church of Maria in Pirna too, the steep hipped roof contrasts to the three-aisled late Gothic interior space. This dissimilarity seems to us less marked, however, perhaps because the image is so familiar or because the roof is primarily seen at a distance.

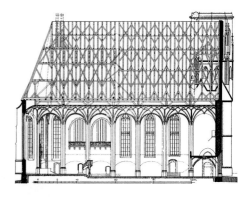

Independence

Building volume and interior space demonstrate a certain autonomy which is facilitated by a mitigating interstice between the two. In the theater in Lelystad, there is an atmospheric and formal correlation between interior and exterior, but there is no direct relation on the interior to the roof. In the House in White, tension is created by developing the living spaces independent from the roof. The last space, however, extends directly up to the roof skin so that the relationship between volume and interior becomes transparent.

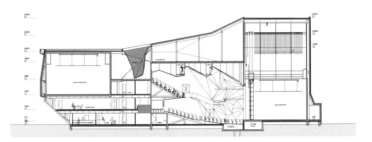

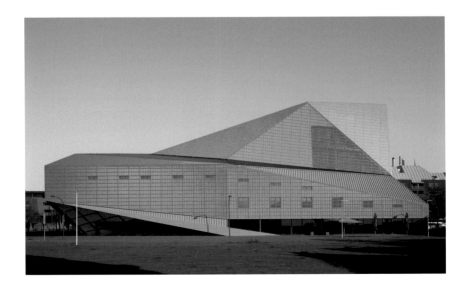

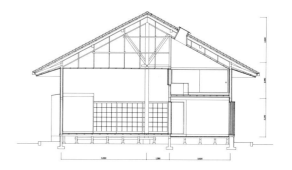

External and Internal Silhouette
Remarks on Poché, on Pink in Section
Jacques Lucan

If one raises the question of the relationship between section and roof in a building, one might find an introduction to the topic in an article by Jacques-François Blondel, whose *Cours d'architecture* was one of the most important architectural texts to appear in the second half of the 18th century. For the design of the abbey-church for the royal abbey of Saint-Louis in Metz,[1] Blondel drew a section in 1763 that offers insights into a series of clearly distinguished components of a building or a space: portico, nave, altar space, choir and gallery. The individual parts differ from one another so greatly in spatial form and height, roof form and lighting that the whole seems like a collage of heterogeneous elements. It is not easy to understand the volumetric character of the whole, so different are the parts. The plan of the abbey church, on the other hand, seems much more compact. The disproportion between section and plan reveals more than the independence of the parts: it demands a plausible synthesis between interior and exterior. At stake here is a compositional problem that the 19th century tried to solve.

Internal Silhouette – External Silhouette

The section reveals what some might call the building's silhouette. If considering the building's exterior, it is the external silhouette; if considering a sequence of spaces, which can be varied in height and form, then it is the internal silhouette. Between internal and external silhouette, there can be a deviation, an interstice. This interstice must not be apparent. The fact that the internal and external silhouettes of a building deviate can be concealed from perception and remain undetectable. In short, the two silhouettes must not correspond.

In the case of the dome in the seating area of the Paris Opera (see p. 138), this is completely understandable. Even if Charles Garnier said of his building that "the external building volume, the form of the exterior, allows for deduction about the internal complex, the form of its interior."[2] That does not change the fact that there is an enormous void between the ceiling of the seating area and the dome's exterior skin arching above it. This void is not functionally urgently needed, but in consideration of the Opera's importance in the cityscape and the representation of its components, it is indispensable. While the building was under construction, some criticized what they considered the over-dimensioned dome or the disproportion between interior and exterior; it was even descried as deception.

In light of the discrepancy between internal and external silhouette, it is fair to ask about the volatile relationship between a building's content and expression. It is a question which modern architecture attempted to answer, in, among other ways, the famous maxim *form follows function*. The question of this discrepancy also raises the question of poché.

Poché

The term "poché" derives from the vocabulary of the Parisian École des Beaux-Artes as it was used in the 19th and early 20th century. The expression was applied in the daily jargon of the atelier and was, although only sparsely and much later, adopted by texts by architects and architectural theoreticians.

In the case of a presentation drawing of a plan, poché referred to the color, usually black, used to represent the thickness of a wall cut at one meter above the floor level. In the case of a construction drawing used on the job site to give information about the constructional character of a wall, color was left out or only a light color was used. Poché can also be found in section although less frequently in black, since the intention there is less to reiterate the spatial boundary than to focus attention on the expanse of the interior spaces.

By virtue of the poché, two antithetical construction principles become accessible. Poché is particularly common in solid wall construction; the poché of the walls clarifies the circumscription of space so that the respective spatial form is obvious at first glance. In concrete frame construction, with its regularly spaced columns, on the other hand, poché is not found. An early example of the application of reinforced concrete frame construction is the Perret Brothers' Théâtre des Champs-Elysées, about which

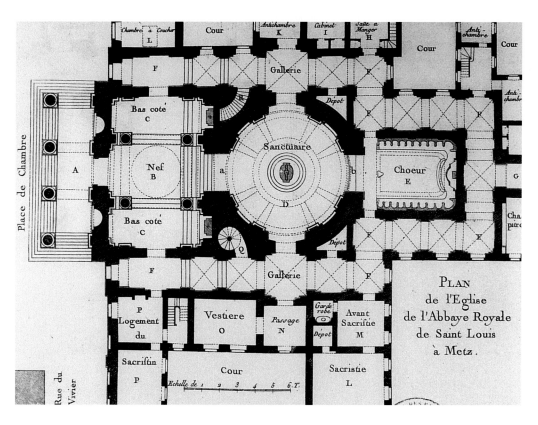

Jacques-François Blondel, Church at the Royal Abbey of
Saint-Lous in Metz, 1763; section and plan.

Charles Garnier, Paris Opera, 1875;
longitudinal and lateral sections.

Paul Guadet enthused in his 1913 article for the journal *L'Architecte,* "At no point do I see solid walls; where are the resplendent 'poché spaces' which indicate superpositioning and massaged solutions? [...] No, there are neither 'poché spaces' nor overly clever spatial solutions, because the elegant building composition allowed by reinforced concrete can do without them[...]."[3]

Relative to Henri Labrouste's interest in issues of construction, the architectural historian Pierre Saddy has noted that the builder of the Bibliothèque Sainte-Geneviève and the Bibliothèque nationale was particularly interested in thickness, in other words, in the pink areas of the section drawing, another variation of poché. The pink color used in section was "a color which was usually applied with watercolor on paper or with color pencil on blueprint; in larger scale drawings, so-called construction documents, it was used to indicate the solid parts of a building that had been cut in section (comparable to the flesh-colored skin sections in anatomical drawings)."[4]

The pink in section is thus the color with which sectioned solid elements are filled or rather, the parts of the section which correspond to the thickness of the building if one includes in "thickness" not only solid masonry construction but also the distance between interior spatial boundary and exterior building shell. In other terms, it is the region between internal and external silhouette. Precisely this interstice was occupied by elements which answered to the various demands of, for example, a particular type of construction or of daylighting. In some buildings, one can, upon closer inspection of the pink, make surprising discoveries and unearth unexpected elements. For example, there is nothing in the appearance of Jacques-Germain Soufflot's Church of Sainte-Geneviève in Paris, now known as the Panthéon (see p. 140), to indicate that the architect had used arched buttresses to support the vault's thrust. Here, one finds a new perspective on the constructional elements which are known from countless examples from the Middle Ages. In order to recognize and understand his recourse to this buttress form, one has to look carefully at the build-ing's lateral section and comprehend those elements which remain concealed from the eye. These are the elements which correspond to pink in section.

On the occasions when pink is used as a transparent color layer in section, there is a good reason for it. It is exactly those construction-determined building elements which are to remain still visible. In a section drawing for a court of appeal (see p. 140) with which Labrouste won the first prize of the Prix de Rome in 1824, great care was taken in representing the spaces – entry, corridor, courtroom. The corresponding surfaces are washed in grey, such that scaled grey tones and drawn shading contribute to the depth of space. The cut portions of the building are not so carefully worked: they indicate roof structure, although more as a sketch that cannot compete with the artful representation of the major spaces.

Inasmuch as he was interested in the thickness of things and thus in pink in section, Henri Labrouste focused his interest, according to Pierre Saddy, on that which one "had until then left to the builder,"[5] on the structure underlying the spatial boundary, the spanning floors or the domes. It is legitimate to ask whether it is not because of this interest in pink that Labrouste developed unusual and original construction solutions for the roof of the reading room in the Bibliothèque Sainte-Geneviève and Nationale. These were solutions which probed the architectural form of metal structural construction, in other words, of constructional solutions which had nothing to do with those of solid masonry construction.

The Slow Disappearance of Poché ...

In order to return to the question of the distance between internal and external silhouette, might it no be possible to establish the hypothesis that the elimination of this distance through the conformity or even the complete confluence of both silhouettes represents an ideal solution?

In this sense, one might understand the roof garden, the third of the "five points towards a new architecture" as formulated by Le Corbusier in 1927, not only as a compensation for or even a doubling of the lost

Jacques-Germain Soufflot, Panthéon, Paris;
section through the dome.

Henri Labrouste, Courthouse; section.
Submission for the Grand Prix 1824.

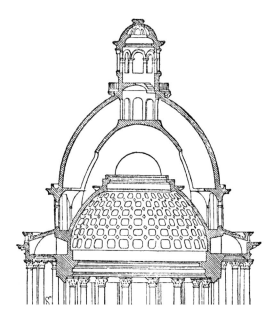

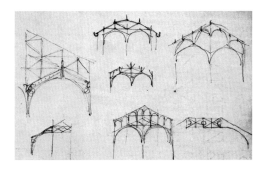

Henri Labrouste, Bibliothèque Sainte-Geneviève, Paris; first sketch of the spanning structure above the reading room.

Bibliothèque Sainte-Geneviève, Paris.

Henri Labrouste, Bibliothèque nationale, Paris; view into the Reading Room.

space under the roof by virtue of the roof terrace. One might also see it as the elimination of a space seen as useless: the attic, used by tenants for storage or as a living space, leading to the creation of the roof dormers and other protrusions so hated by Le Corbusier. In the case of the roof garden, interior and exterior are only separated by a plane – a concrete slab, of course, since "it is thanks to reinforced concrete that the flat roof and the revolutionary reuse of the house are possible."[6] Reinforced concrete also meant "liberation from centuries-old dictates."[7]

Others dreamed of an even more radical elimination of the distance between inside and outside by thinking it in purely virtual terms, to the extreme of envisioning life in a bubble with a controlled atmosphere in which existence within complete transparency would be possible. One of them was Reyner Banham. For him, it was vital to differentiate between two contradictory models of which one stood for the traditional architectural values whereas the other aimed at the dematerialization of architecture. In his 1969 book *The Architecture of the Well-tempered Environment,* he juxtaposes shelter to the open fire. Using the example of a primitive tribe, which comes to the place at which its temporary lodgings for the night are to be set up and where wood is plentiful, he formulates the following alternative: "Two basic methods of exploiting the environmental potential of that timber exist: either it may be used to construct a wind-break or rain-shed – the structural solution – or it may be used to build a fire – the power-operated solution."[8] Here, two cultures are juxtaposed: the one forms its environment by means of massive structures with which an understanding of space is allied "which is bounded and closed by virtue of walls, floors, ceilings."[9] The other distinguishes itself by virtue of the way in which life turns about a center – be it a spring, a tree, a fire or a master around which or whom all collect in order to belong – in which a "space, defined by functional demands, whose external boundaries are rather vague and therefore seldom regular."[10] It is understandable that the issue of the distance between internal and external silhouette and of the relationship between them would become immaterial in the case of this latter hypothesis. The thickness of poché or of pink in section has, then, vanished, has removed itself, is simply gone.

… and the Return of Poché

Still, there is an architect who rediscovered the virtues of poché: Louis I. Kahn. The American architect who had trained in the tradition of the École des Beaux-Artes in Paris, was familiar with the term "poché"; it is also found, for example, in a glossary written in 1922 by Raymond Hood, one of the architects of Rockefeller Center in New York, for the journal *Pencil Points.* Hood defined certain terms that were common in studio jargon, including: "Poche: the walls of a plan blackened in; fig., the study of a plan with reference to the walls and piers only."[11] The term was of course not applied only to plan but also to section.

Kahn rediscovered the advantages of poché while developing his theory of the hollow column,[12] through which he again lent thickness to the space-enveloping shell with absolute consistency. The intention was to create a place for all systems which were necessary for comfort and natural lighting: "I thought of a support as being a hollow column which can be used […] so the source of support, the column, became the place which harbored the services of the building."[13] The principle of the hollow column is not limited to the vertical; regardless of dimension, poché can contribute to the definition of any space. It pinpoints the opposition between servant and served spaces.

Is this retrograde? At least, it is revisionist: a critical examination, which would have extensive consequences for architecture. The final discussion on this topic deals with Rem Koohaas. He, too, has developed his own definition of poché. He did this initially implicitly, inasmuch as he systematically represented many of his projects almost symmetrically in black and white – although black and white were interchangeable. The intention was to make obvious the relation between different, if comparable, elements of a building program. One excellent example is the plans and sections for the competition entry to the French National Library (1989). The opposition of black and white corresponds here to the publicly accessible spaces and the library stacks: "the library is understood as a solid block of information, as a place in which all possible kinds of memory-storage is located: books, images, microfiche, computer … In this block, public spaces are understood as an absence of the built, as hollows in the solid block of information."[14]

Ten years later, in the Casa da Música de Porto (1999 – 2004), the hollowed public spaces recur, particularly the large auditorium, in opposition to the servant spaces which create the subordinate thickness. These are hollows – and poché. And if one can, in this case, speak of poché, then not least of all because Koolhaas himself ascribed value to the insight that "it was fascinating to work for the first time with so-called poché"[15] – even if it was of course not the first time.

1   See Jacques-François Blondel, "Suite de l'expérience de l'art, où l'on rapporte divers exemples d'édifices sacrés, de la composition de l'auteur", in: Blondel, *Cours d'architecture,* Vol. III, Paris 1772, Ch. VII, Plate LX (Plan of
    the church for the royal abbey of Saint-Louis in Metz) and Plate LXI (Section).
2   Charles Garnier, *Le Théâtre,* Paris 1871, p. 402.
3   Paul Guadet, "Le théâtre des Champs-Elysées", in: *L'Architecte,* 1913, p. 74.
4   Pierre Saddy, "Henri Labrouste architecte-constructeur", in: *Les Monuments historiques de la France,* No. 6, 1975.
5   Ibid.
6   Le Corbusier, "Calendrier d'architecture", in: *Almanach d'architecture moderne,* Paris 1926, p. 14.
7   Ibid., p. 15
8   Reyner Banham, The Architecture of the Well-Tempered Environment, Chicago 1969, p. 19.
9   Banham, *The Architecture of the Well-Tempered Environment,* op. cit, p. 21.
10 Ibid., p. 20
11 Raymond M. Hood, "A Vocabulary of Atelier French", in *Pencil Points,* April to October 1922.
12 William H. Jordy, "Kahn on Beaux-Arts Training", in: The Architectural Review, Vol. 155, No. 928, June 1974.
13 John W. Cook/Heinrich Klotz, *Conversations with Architects,* New York 1973, p. 215.
14 Patrice Goulet (ed.), *OMA – Rem Koolhaas. Six Projets,* Paris/Rome 1990, p. 295.
15 Rem Koolhaas, "Transformations", in: *A + U,* Special Issue OMA @work.a+u, May 2000, p. 110.

Louis I. Kahn, Library, Phillips Exeter Academy in Exeter, 1971; section.

OMA – Rem Koolhaas, Competition project for the Bibliothèque nationale de France, Paris, 1989; section through the building and plan of the sixteenth storey, showing the black (poché) of the book stacks and the white areas of the different publicly accessible spaces.

OMA – Rem Koolhaas, Casa da Música, Porto; schematic plans.

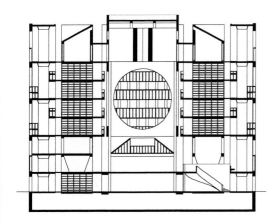

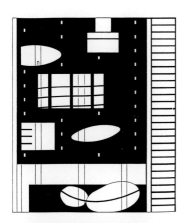

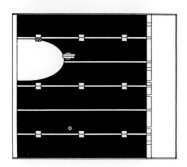

Spaces Beneath the Roof

Spaces Beneath the Roof

The perception of spaces with flat ceilings is determined by the vertical walls, while the horizontal planes of ceiling and floor emphasize their connection to other spaces. If the ceiling is sloped, it moves into the perceptual range of the standing person and binds itself much more forcefully with the walls to form a unit which differentiates itself from the floor. Bettina Köhler notes astutely in her essay, "The – visible – roof [...] individualizes and concentrates forcefully, whereas the [flat] ceiling, on the other hand, insures the continuity within a building's interior."

Ceilings which evoke or make visible the roof were mostly used in important spaces within the history of architecture, or in spaces which were intended to acquire meaning by virtue of this move. The concentrating or inclusive power of roofs was particularly used to create a space for people to gather, be it for religious, cultural or political reasons. The inhabitation in the roof, or the explicit use of the roof space for private quarters, has only been a topic in architecture since the 19th century.

For the most part, the rule holds: "one space – one roof." But there are examples in which the roof contains several spaces or in which a space can be subdivided into portions. On the other hand, one can observe the phenomenon that a small portion of the roof revealed in one space can refer to the roof as a whole.

A roof can have a concentrating effect on a space, but also a dynamic one: it can give it orientation, breadth or constraint. Since, as Jakob Burkhardt put it, "forms have been set in motion,"[1] it seems natural to us to use active vocabulary to describe architecture although, of course, neither space nor spatial container move. It is much more a matter of "the subject's activity, [...] who immediately transposes his own feeling of movement to the static spatial form [...] or attributes to immobile lines, planes and volumes the movement that his eyes and his muscular senses indicate to him [...]."[2] Oblique planes in particular have this effect, and pitched roofs are different again from walls that are oblique in plan but stand perpendicular to the floor. That is because, while the latter evoke the movement of a subject in space, sloped roofs refer primarily to gravity, which effects architecture and subject alike. Tension – or the sense of dynamism – arises here from the fact that the sloped roof surfaces seem simultaneously to move upwards and, in conformity to gravity, downwards.[3]

In the essay, "The Tent Room: the Magical 'Image of the Whole Space'", Bettina Köhler deals with an architectural phenomenon of the late 18th century. What at first appears to be a curiosity from a long-past era reveals itself in her description to be a kind of essence of the roof space. It is here that the roof and wall, by virtue of their synergy, achieve a particularly intensive spatial effect or, in fact, an "image of the whole space." In that way, the tent room can be seen as a precursor of current tendencies to eliminate completely the differentiation of floor, wall and roof and, by virtue of the oblique as all-encompassing space-defining plane, to lend the space dynamism. The result is to overcome gravity and to take the weight away from the architecture. It is a goal which the tent room achieved in a remarkably playful manner.

Barbara Burren

1   Jakob Burckhardt, *Der Cicerone,* Reproduction of the original edition, Stuttgart 1978.
2   August Schmarsow, *Das Wesen der architektonischen Schöpfung*, Leipzig 1894, p. 19.
3   Rudolf Arnheim, "Das Bauwerk als Anschauung", in: *Daidalos*, No. 67, 1998, p. 28.

Centering

The roof form can contribute to the centering of a space. The dome of Hagia Sophia arches above the enormous church space and simultaneously focuses it on its center. The space of the Small Palace of Sports in Rome recalls a clam, with its long-span, flat arch and shell-shaped stands; it binds spectators and athletes into a single whole. The concrete structure in the roof space of the Tanzhaus in Zurich creates a kind of mirror vault and thus lends the space a tranquil character although it is at the same time connected to the exterior by large apertures. In the Studio in Karuizawa, the roof, which spans across the living room like an umbrella, evokes in its dialogue with the powerful central hearth the impression of shelter and comfort.

Pier Luigi Nervi **Kursaal, Ostia, 1950**
Toyo Ito **Funeral Hall, Kagamihara, 2006**
Eugenio Montuori et.al **Stazione Termini, Rome, 1951**
Ernst Gisel **Sculpture Studio, Zurich, 1954**

The umbrella-like roof at the Kursaal in Lido di Ostia is the antithesis of a dome. Beginning from the central column, the space moves outwards on all sides. In the funeral hall in Kagamihara, on the other hand, the columns which emerge from the roof eaves reach down to connect interior and exterior as well as above and below. With a generous gesture of the wavy roof, the long hall of the Stazione Termini in Rome is spatially bounded but also oriented towards the exit side. The space thus acquires a sense of dynamism, which pushes the travelers coming from the trains into the city. In the sculpture studio in Zurich, a slight lift in the roof's north edge is enough to create tension in the otherwise stabile space.

Lifting Up and Weighing Down

Jørn Utzon   **Private House, Herning, 1967**
Kenzo Tange   **Small Olympic Hall, Tokyo, 1964**
Le Corbusier   **Chapel, Ronchamps, 1954**
Alejandro de la Sota   **Gynasium Colegio Maravillas, Madrid, 1961**

In the house in Herning, originally planned as a school, the space between the two arched, almost volumetric roof planes seems to open upwards towards the light, and in the Olympic Hall in Tokyo, the space even seems to surge upwards. The actual height of the space can only be inferred from the light falling from above and the rising roof structure. The dark ceiling of the chapel of Ronchamp gives the impression of a heavy cloth which hangs down into the space, while the space-containing roof of the gymnasium of the Colegio Maravillas pushes into the space from above, like a powerful volume.

Articulating and Binding

The roof can bind together different spaces to make a single space or, vice versa, can articulate a single space into subspaces. In the Leibundgut House in Uhwiesen, the pitched roof follows the terraced terrain and unites the spaces, which are all at different ground levels. The folded roof of House F in Shina-

gawa, on the other hand, develops independently of the complex domestic landscape below it and thus becomes the characteristic element of the house. The reading room in the Bibliothèque Sainte Geneviève in Paris is subdivided in two zones by its thin columns, but more importantly, by the two barrel vaults running longitudinally. In the Church la Milagrosa in Narvarte, the expressively folded concrete roof articulates the space along its length into nave and aisles but at the same time also defines cross-axes. It thus acts both to articulate and to bind.

Part and Whole

Atelier Bow-Wow **Saiko House, Ashiwada, 2002**
Lux Guyer **Saffa House, Zurich/Stäfa, 1928**
OMA **Casa da Música, Porto, 2005**

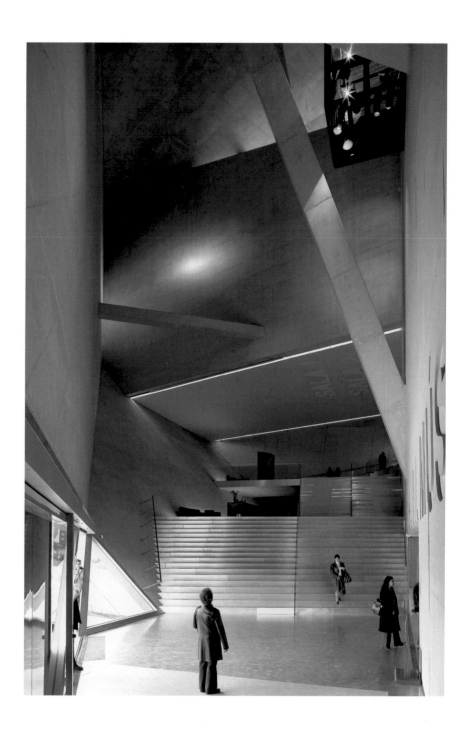

Although it is not signaled by a special material, the oblique planes in the bathroom of the Saiko House are immediately recognizable as quadrants of the roof which reference the roof space with their geometry. In the Saffa House, the oblique planes make the space of the roof legible as such, but their rela- tion to the roof as a whole remains ambiguous since the suggestive oblique planes are used freely to define space. In the Casa da Música in Porto, too, the oblique planes on the interior reference the exterior form, although here, it is the entire envelope and not only the roof that comprises obliques.

Spaces Beneath the Roof
Roof, Wall and Floor

The relationship between ceiling, wall and floor is decisive for the effect of spaces beneath the roof. In the Garden Center in Camorino, the space stretches between floor and shell-like roof, and thus communicates both a sense of shelter and an impression of expanse. Comfort dominates in the Trigon House near Brig, on the other hand, in the way the roof stretches to the floor, and in the Dolder House, in which the wall seamlessly melds with the roof. It is different at the Chapel Sogn Benedetg, in which the sheltering roof is separated from the walls and seems to expand the space upwards.

Heinz Isler   **Garden Center, Camorino, 1973**
Heidi and Peter Wenger   **Trigon House, Brig, 1955**
Peter Vetsch   **Dolder House, Widen, 1989**
Peter Zumthor   **Chapel Sogn Benedetg, Somvix, 1988**

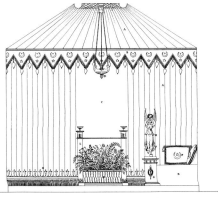

Berthault, Tent room boudoir of Princess de Courlande, 1787.

K.F. Schinkel, Tent Room, Charlottenhof, Potsdam.
Watercolor, after 1830.

Tent Room
The Magical "Image ot the Entire Space"
Bettina Köhler

Prologue: Tent. Room. Fashion.

Since the late 1870s, tent rooms were built in European palaces, villas and city residences – a fashion which only dissipated slowly fifty years later in order to experience a comeback, under an entirely different star, in the hippie culture of the late 1970s. Tent rooms were in the time of their invention extravagant formulations of a luxurious (but not necessarily only aristocratic) domestic culture. The fact that they could play equally upon the traditions of European or Ottoman military tents and with those of festival culture meant that they seemed equally appropriate to demonstrate military austerity as they are to celebrate luxury. The boudoir, the bedroom, the guest room and even the representative *Salle du Conseil* could be designed as tent room. The decision on whether this particular tent room should seem simple or rather luxurious seems to have been essential. Less decisive was whether the ornament, patterns, carpets and not least of all the type of drapery tend more towards Turkish or Roman or simply generally exotic.

Far beyond contemporary stylistic interpretations of the tent room as Empire style,[1] these rooms are above all remarkable as architectural manifestations of a particular spatial understanding: the walls of the tent room were not bounded by a ceiling which corresponded to the ceiling of the adjacent rooms, but rather by a roof, a singular, textile tent roof. Its representation in architectural compendia proceeded such that the entire "tent" was executed with walls and roof, contrary to the representation of traditional spaces in which wall and ceiling were separate drawings. One might also say: in tent rooms, it was a persuasive architectural synthesis that was at stake. Apertures such as windows, doors and hearths as well as furniture, paintings and mirrors, to the extent that the latter were desirable, had to be unified persuasively with the presence of the tent and with the strong "combinatory" effect of the roof. Consequently, in most cases, the entire furnishings of the room were designed expressively for it. And here precisely lay the architectural potential of the tent room, namely, the capacity to seem modern in a "romantic way". By means of the tent room, the "image of the room" was designed, a modern architectural theme which had been formulated as the theoretical consideration of affect and presence since the 18th century, if at first only sparsely.[2] In the tent room, this consideration manifested itself concretely and in a "romantic way" because it intended to achieve ambiguous effects, which also imply ideas of transgressed boundaries. In the tent room, one was – seemingly – on the road: far away, in an army camp, but simultaneously, in a stable building.

1. Scene: the Watercolor of the Tent Room

The view into the tent room at Charlottenhof Castle, the summer residence of Crown Prince Friedrich Wilhlem IV and his wife Crown Princess Elisabeth, as painted in watercolors by an anonymous observer in 1830, still retains a fairytale-like quality. The painting tries to make us nearly forget the fact that we as viewers are standing at the room's threshold, in other words, inside the little castle. The watercolor invites us to imagine that the tent were located in the open air. The fact that this is an illusion is clearly indicated in the representation but equally, that this illusion is at stake, the "as-if". That is precisely the reason why the watercolorist decided to show a portion of the adjacent room, the maid's room, through the door opening; one sees a bit of wall, mirror and wood furniture. Thus, the particular character of the tent room as distinct from that of the typical interior furnishings of that period is made so much the clearer.[3]

2. Scene: a Photograph of a Tent Room in Comparison to the Watercolor

It is legitimate to assume that the representation closely approximates the architect's intentions regarding the effect of the space if one looks at a modern photograph of the actual room. The view through the window to the surrounding park is integral to the games of illusion: Schinkel reveals the architecture of the window, which is part of the real architecture, and this strategy demands that one accepts both at once: that one is in a tent and in a room, which is a part of a domestic architectural work. The consistency with which Schinkel realized the tent in the house and at the same time alternated between the two planes – picturesque illusion and "real" artifact – is evident in the materials used: blue and white striped wallpaper instead of the respective textiles denotes the tent's walls, just as the spatial boundary above, fashioned from linen, signifies the roof of the tent. The green painted center pole and the horizontal cross pole of this roof are, on the other hand, really made of metal. And the baldachin above the iron bed, held in place by crossed lances, the bed curtains, the curtains at the windows and doors, and the upholstery on the iron chair designed especially for the room are made out of blue and white striped drill. The room's floor, as the watercolor shows, was originally covered with linoleum without a border, just as in the other rooms of the castle the floor was covered with oilcloth of different colors and patterns. In the "fictional" tent room, the grass green paint and the floral pattern of the linoleum recall the fact that a real tent must be pitched by bounding an area of the natural ground and raising a framework for the tent fabric. At the same time, however, the entire construct denotes the carpet as the textile floor of a real tent. In the famous tapestry, now in the Musée de Cluny in Paris, entitled *The Lady and the Unicorn,* the lady's tent is pitched on a field of flowers, although the representation remains notably ambiguous about whether we are seeing a real meadow or a carpet with a floral pattern whose edge is curled up.

As much as there was a constant change in reference in Schinkel's tent room between the levels of house and tent architecture, between illusion and reality, the consequence for the whole design however was a new, more radical effect in comparison to earlier tent rooms.

Intermezzo: Tent and Tent Room

"Several, but at least three conically placed posts or poles create the simplest, spatially stable construction. In order to create a bounded space, this skeleton or construction should be clad with several or fewer stretched envelopes."[4] A glance at the history of the tent shows that, next to the "simplest" construction made of three poles, many different possibilities existed (and still exist) to define the space of a tent. Two types in particular, however, experienced a golden age in the Ottoman Empire in both military and civilian applications: the round tent with a domed or station roof, and the rectangular pavilion with gabled roof. The tents looted during the Ottoman wars, which served first as festival architecture and were recreated in park complexes,[5] represented possible precedents for the beloved tent room. The same is true of the European military tent tradition so well known from paintings of often quite splendid army camps.

One of the first tent rooms was created as a bedroom for the Comte d'Artois, the youngest brother of Louis XVI, in 1777 by François Joseph Bélanger in the Bagatelle Castle near Paris. Shortly before the turn of the century, the architect Friedrich Gilly praised the "painterly effect" of the tent interior in his essays on architecture, which discussed, among other buildings, the Bagatelle Castle.[6] A few years later, in 1801, Krafft and Rasonette published the tent room boudoir for Princess Courlande, realized by Berthault in 1787. And around the same time, Percier and Fontaine's publication in their compendium of the *Salle du Conseil* of the Malmaison Castle near Paris (1799) introduced it to a wide audience. The room was installed for Napoleon after the model of a "rich" commander's tent.[7] From then on, the "tent room" type belonged to the repertoire of possible spatial forms for the next forty years. Of modern spatial forms.

3. Scene: Other Tent Rooms. A Comparison.

Crown Prince Friedrich William himself commissioned "the decoration of the corner room for court women using tent-like wall papers and similar drapery"[8] in 1829. How far he went in determining colors and patterns, and whether the prince himself suggested the pear-like form of the gabled roof, is no longer clear; a corresponding perspective drawing has vanished.[9] The fact that Schinkel interpreted the "simple" tent room in new ways by means of colors, materials and forms, and thus interpreted the military

The Lady and the Unicorn, Tapestry, 1480–1500.

K.F. Schinkel, the Tent Room in Charlottenhof, Potsdam.

François-Joseph Bélanger, Tent Room in Bagatelle,
Paris, 1775; elevation of the fireplace wall, watercolored
pen drawing.

Percier et Fontaine, Salle du Conseil, Château de Malmaison, Paris, 1799.

Tent Room in an English country house, early 1830s.

background of the "simple language" in a less anecdotal and more functional manner, becomes clear in comparison to the earlier formulations already mentioned.

The bedroom of the Comte d'Artois was conceived as a "military tent room", but given its complex drapery and elegant, custom designed furniture, it seems rather to conform to the expectations of a royal bedroom conceived in informal terms.[10] Bundles of lances and other similar martial attributes only served to denote anecdotally the "military" meaning of this tent room: they refer to the occupant's rank as *Grand Maître de l'Artillerie*. Bélanger therefore spanned the long space, outfitted with blue-white stripped tent elements, luxuriously with a roof, which – in a reference to a bell tower roof – rose dome-like for three-quarters of its height with complexly folded drapery and was held in place by a gable roof, tautly spanned with the same striped fabric.

Percier and Fontaine created a splendid commander's tent with their famous *Salle du Conseil*; its black, gold and broken white striped fabric represents a tautly spanned tent wall and an equally taut, flat gabled roof. The decorations – door flaps painted with Antique warriors, gilded eagles on mahogany columns between the doors, a gilt "tent post" at the roof – reference the military background of Napoleon's regime, among other things. This décor is simultaneously a narrative bearer of meaning and also a manifold system of articulating the tent architecture. A preciously framed fireplace and mirror leave no doubt, however, that in this tent, one is actually in a representative building.

Both of the tent rooms described are so conceived with concern for elegance, comfort and representation that the design of the tent, as well as the furniture despite all exotica or one-off's, approaches traditional spatial formulations. In another tent room, still extant today in an English country house, it is the station roof that exemplifies how it is possible to use the gradation of color relative to the wall covering, as well as complex drapery, to lend the space a festive character, intimate and yet also exotic. At the same time, the fireplace with mirror and the various paintings speak to traditional ideas of furnishings and decoration.

It is entirely different in the case of the Charlottenhof tent room. Schinkel, in his interpretation of the crown prince's wishes, used the function of the court ladies' room to turn the appropriate simplicity of the space into architectural capital. The fact that this room was used as a guest room as well – Schinkel himself as well as Alexander von Humboldt slept here – speaks for the fact that a particular formulation within the series of European tent rooms was successfully realized in Potsdam.

The potential of the tent room, noted at the outset, to stand as a witness to modernity is exploited here fully. The articulating elements are limited to the minimum necessary and the drapery is rather "quoted [as a] frozen form" than voluptuously draped. In this space, not a single painting hangs, and that, in a house, which is otherwise filled with decisively located paintings. Schinkel creates an "empty" space and thus the "picture of the whole space". The space is spare and simultaneously rich in what it offers: to be a traveler in a tent, to "wander in ones own imagination". Schinkel's tent room demonstrates how the romantic search for transgression of boundaries can be united with the modern search for, as Schinkel put it, truth in construction and functionality.[11] This approach takes equally seriously the demands of perception and the desire for a lively and open space, in other words, the necessary illusion of effect and the concrete reality of the artifact.

Postscript: Gottfried Semper. William Morris.

The fact that Gottfried Semper based his claim for the textile origins of architecture[12] and the consequent distinction between vestment and construction upon the Caribbean hut[13] and not upon the tent seems at first surprising. In the case of the tent, however – or so it is safe to assume – the differentiation between vestment and construction in architecture cannot be as persuasively demonstrated: the tent's roof, like the image of the Assyrian dome tent noted by Semper, is formally and materially identical inside and out.[14] Beginning with the image of the hut,

John Nash, Royal Pavillion, Brighton, 1811–1820.

Philip Webb, Red House, Work room of William Morris, upper floor, Bexleheath near London, 1859.

however, Semper can maintain the following for architecture: beneath the roof construction, a ceiling acts as the vestment for the construction since this horizontal (or arched) ceiling is the conclusion of the space as it is intended to be perceived.[15]

The – visible – roof, even the tent roof of a tent room, individualizes and concentrates forcefully, whereas the ceiling, on the other hand, insures the continuity within a building's interior. Perhaps this is the reason that the fashion of the tent room gathered force in revolutionary times as a singular statement and then disappeared with the return to the conventional. This remains, however, speculation. In architecture historical terms, it seems significant that this fashion occurred on the threshold of an era in which the criterion of a connection between interior and exterior become increasingly important in parallel to the desire to configure space. It was also an era in which the roof acquired a decisive role.[16] Philip Webb realized precisely such a house with his 1859 Red House in Bexleheath near London, in which the roofscape implies the spaces lodged beneath it. William Morris, the client, had planned from the outset to use the attic space as studio and drawing room, in other words, as significant spaces. The view into his studio shows that the roof construction has remained visible and is even emphasized by the plastered, patterned planes which infill between its members. In a metaphorical sense, one could say: a workroom is located beneath the quadrant of the tent roof. The Red House set off a movement. The roof was discovered and used as a habitable space with special qualities.

One last glance backwards: the Royal Pavilion in Brighton represents the realization of an architecture ensemble that in section insinuates the idea of a tent colony, comprising three large tent rooms (see p. 166/167). Said in modern terms: in Brighton, we have an architectural ensemble in which interior and exterior were supposed to correspond vibrantly. It is not only in the Red House that this idea was taken up and concretized: perhaps the magical fashion of the tent room effected more than one commonly supposes.

1 For example, see: Karin Harather, *Haus-Kleider. Zum Phänomen der Bekleidung in der Architektur,* Wien/Köln/Weimar 1995, p. 63, or in: Alan & Ann Gore, *The History of English Interiors,* London 1995, p. 109. General information on the style of drapery in interiors ca. 1800 and on the fashion of the tent room in particular relative to another design by Schinkel, see: Adelheid Schendel, "Anmerkungen zu einem Musselinkabinett der Königin Luise im Kronprinzenpalais in Berlin", in: Hans Dickel et al. (Eds.), *Preußen, die Kunst und das Individuum – Beiträge für Helmut Börsch Supan,* Berlin 2003, pp. 150 ff.

2 Bettina Köhler, "Architekturgeschichte als Geschichte der Raumwahrnehmung (Architecture History as the History of Spatial Experience)", in: *Daidalos,* No. 67, 1998, pp. 36–43. Bettina Köhler, "Alle Sinne in Bewegung – Zum Beginn einer Diskussion über Körper und Raum in der Architektur", in: Ingeborg Flagge (Eds.), *Jahrbuch Licht und Architektur, Architektur und Wahrnehmung,* Darmstadt 2003, pp. 20–27.

3 The tent room was installed in the small palace in 1829 at the request of the Crown Prince, see: Heinz Schönemann, *Karl Friedrich Schinkel. Charlottenhof Potsdam-Sanssouci,* Stuttgart/London 1997, pp. 16. And: *Karl Friedrich Schinkel 1781–1841,* exhibition catalogue, Potsdam 1981, pp. 187 ff. Also: Elke Katharina Wittich, "Das Schloss Charlottenhof in Potsdam", in: Bärbel Hedinger/Julia Berger, *Karl Friedrich Schinkel. Möbel und Interieurs,* Hamburg 2002, p. 164.

4 Berthold Burckhardt quoted in Harather, *Haus-Kleider – Zum Phänomen der Bekleidung in der Architektur,* op. cit., p. 62 f. General information on the tent: Philipp Drew, *Tensile Architecture,* London 1979.

5 Rainer Graefe, "Textile Schmuckformen an Fassaden + Dächern", in: *Daidalos,* No. 29, 1988, p. 87 f.

6 See Schendel, "Anmerkungen zu einem Musselinkabinett der Königin Luise im Kronprinzenpalais in Berlin", op. cit., p. 157. Fritz Neumeyer (Ed.), *Friedrich Gilly, Essays über Architektur [1796–1799],* Berlin 1997, p. 160.

7 Charles Percier, *P. F. L. Fontaine, Recueil de Décorations Intérieurs,* Paris 1801, Plate 55.

8 Schönemann, *Karl Friedrich Schinkel. Charlottenhof Potsdam-Sanssouci,* op. cit., p. 187.

9 Ibid., p. 187 f.

10 François Scherrer, "La Chambre à coucher du Comte d'Artois à Bagatelle d'aprés les documents des Archives Nationales," in: *Gazette des Beaux Arts,* January, 1985, p. 147.

11 See several points in: Goerd Peschken/Margharete Kühn (Eds.), *Karl Friedrich Schinkel. Das Architektonische Lehrbuch,* Berlin 1979.

12 "[…] it is certain that *the beginning of building coincides with the beginning of textiles."* Gottfried Semper, *Style in the Technical and Tectonic Arts,* Vol. 1, Los Angeles 2004, p. 247 (Translation: Harry Francis Mallgrave and Michael Robinson)

13 Gottfried Semper, *Der Stil in den technischen und tektonischen Künsten,* Vol 2, Frankfurt/M. 1860, p. 666.

14 Ibid. pp. 293 f.

15 Ibid., p. 65.

16 See Edward Hollamby, *Arts and Crafts Houses I: Red House,* London 1999.

Roof and Structure

Roof and Structure

There is an enormous wealth of publications on structure and construction of pitched roofs, which tend to focus on technical rather than architectural questions. This reflects the current situation in the building disciplines: the structure of the roof is seldom a theme in itself and often disappears entirely in the roof space behind the cladding.

We are concerned here with the roof's structure, which unlike the situation described above, remains visible and thus architecturally effective. As Nott Caviezel explains, open roof structures have been used not for economic reasons, but rather were generated by formal intentions since the early medieval period. They were implemented to distinguish a unified space and to support the concentrated effect of the roof as container of space (see chapter "Spaces Beneath the Roof").

The examples demonstrate that the structure is an effective means even in the present to strengthen the effect of roof spaces, especially when the forms of the structure and space harmonize. If structure and space deviate from each other, on the other hand, ambiguous spatial situations can be generated.

Nott Caviezel's essay "The Open Roof Structure as Symbolic Space" is concerned with medieval churches and halls, but it describes phenomena which remain operable even today for the effect of roof structures. At the heart of this argument is the idea that the structure can transcend itself and become a symbol. In the process, its bearing function and use retreat into the background, while the foreground is occupied by its meaning. A comparable phenomenon can be observed, for example, in the buildings of Kazuo Shinohara: traditional Japanese roof structures are reduced here to their essence and, by virtue of the apparently vanquished static coherence, not as bearing elements but as figures which inhabit the space. These houses also evidence that this kind of bearing structure can be effective not only for large halls, but also for the smallest attic space in a house.

Barbara Burren

Coherence

The structure can emphasize the form of the space beneath the roof and thus strengthen its overall effect. In the Japanese Pavilion in Hanover, the deformations and densification of the regular net-like structure make visible the modulations in lateral section which suggestively zone the space. At the same time, they emphasize the space as a whole and in its depth. In a similar manner, the Priory Chapel in St. Louis is subdivided into individual niches and unified as a central domed space by means of the two-storey shell construction. In the Cuore Immacolato church in Pistoia, the unusual structure in linear rows emphasizes the depth of the space and, by virtue of its form, the asymmetrical, wave-like form of its roof, which lends the space its orientation. In the gymnasium in the Rudolf-Steiner School in Basel, the ornamental effect created by the folded roof conjoins the space into a unified whole, but simultaneously differentiates longitudinal and lateral directions.

Shigeru Ban **Japanese Pavilion, World's Fair Hanover, 2000**
Giovanni Michelucci **Cuore Immacolato di Maria Church, Pistoia, 1961**
HOK **Priory Chapel, St. Louis, 1962**
Hans Felix Leu, Heinz Hossdorf **Gymnasium Rudolf-Steiner School, Basel, 1967**

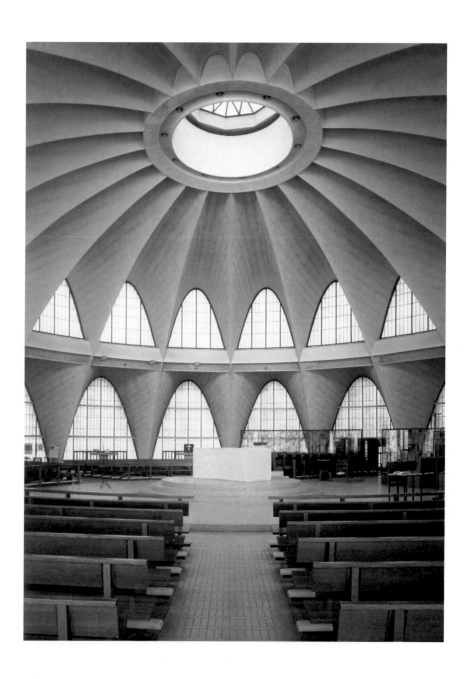

Difference

The spaces defined by roof and structure can deviate from each other, and accordingly, the structure can be more or less forcefully expressed. In the market hall in Wattwil, the timber truss arches create a barrel vault, while the roof and walls formulate a basilica section. In the roof of the Neuwerk church in Goslar, the roof surface creates a tent-like space into which an even more powerful hexagonal space is inscribed by the beams of the roof structure. In the common house of the Seitogakushi School, the effect of a space frame created from raw beams is so dominant that the space-bounding roof behind it almost disappears.

Roof, Structure and Wall

For the effect of the space beneath the roof, it is not only the structure which is important, but the relationship to the wall as well. The roof structure of Santa Croce in Florence is so clearly separated from the masonry wall that the space beneath the roof is perceived as independent. In Westminster Hall in London, roof and wall are integrated by means of pilasters and consoles. In the Torino commodities market building, the connection between roof and wall is even stronger. The ribs of the arched roof seem to grow simultaneously from the columns integrated into the walls. In the Serpentine Gallery pavilion, finally, the difference between wall and ceiling is entirely dissolved.

Figure

Structure can achieve the value of an autonomous sculptural element and figural character. Thus, the light roof structure for the Expo 64 recalls the petal array of a flower, and the trusses in the City Hall of Säynätsalo look like spiders hanging from the ceiling. The slanting struts that grow from the walls in the house in Hanyama become figures in the absence of a larger connection, and the powerful concrete structure of the House in the Curve becomes so abstract that it appears much more like a sculpture than a structure.

Heinz Hossdorf, Florian Vischer **Expo 64, Lausanne, 1964**
Alvar Aalto **City Hall Säynätsalo, 1952**
Kazuo Shinohara **House in Hanayama, Japan, 1968**
Kazuo Shinohara **House in the Curve, Japan, 1978**

Symbol

Structure can indicate much more than itself by virtue of its effect, and recall well-known spatial phenomena: for example, the hull of a ship, as in the Palazzo della Ragione in Padua or a palm grove, as in the Oriente Train Station in Lisbon. Concrete, for example, can seem textile-like and, as in the pilgrimage church in Neviges, recall a tent or, as in the Church of San Giovanni Battista in Florence, a draped cloth.

Giovanni degli Eremitani **Palazzo della Ragione, Padua, 1306**
Santiago Calatrava **Oriente Train Station, Lisbon, 1998**
Giovanni Michelucci **Church of San Giovanni Battista, Florence, 1964**
Gottfried Böhm **Pilgrimage Church Queen of Peace, Neviges, 1972**

Old St.Peter's, Fresco by Filippo Gagliardi
in San Martino ai Monti in Rome, mid 17th Century.

The Open Roof Structure as Symbolic Space

Nott Caviezel

To have a roof over one's head is among the basic human needs. It offers shelter and protection from the climate, and, in folk superstitions, from the evil spirits that like to occupy the space in the beams supporting the roof.[1] The fact that roof and attic like hearth are connected to a number of familiar and yet uncanny fantasies in folk traditions indicates the degree to which these parts of a building play an existential role in concrete daily life as well as in their meaning and interpretation. The roof, appropriately to its primary function, is the most exposed part of a building and consequently fragile. It contains a space that is, as a rule, poorly lit or not lit at all and has not been used on a daily basis for centuries. This was the case for secular buildings until early modern times and only changed in the 17th century with the apotheosis of the mansard roof in which habitable space lit from the side could also be accommodated in the absence of the usual sloping roof planes. As a consequence, the external form and the internal life of the roof lose the innocence of their original, purely practical attribution and the roof gains indicative meaning. More and more, roofs represent something – wealth and power, for example, or technical prowess. On some occasions, they are recognizable, for example, as the roof of an apartment building or a factory. Sometimes, however, they camouflage the life within them, which is often the case with 19th-century historicism and its mask-like formal language. With the first modernist activity, the sense of meaningful forms which allowed the functionally determined roof to be conflated with another, symbolic level, was finally lost. The symbolic values at stake here are not to be confused with the artistically determined expression of a suggestive or mimetic architecture, which draws attention to itself through the use of strong forms and, for example, makes reference to a building's function; this includes dynamic forms used for an airport, or the church that reaches upwards to the heavens to the self-referential constructional acrobatics of the blob. The deeper symbolism of architecture, which today has been largely lost, reflects, finally, the image of a secular society, which has nothing more to do with transcendental or even religious agendas. The relinquishing of certain ideas and orders, which had determined occidental culture for centuries is both a gain and a loss   a gain in terms of formal liberty and a loss of knowledge related to the fundamental iconic language of architecture which, for many years, lent the roof, the attic and the roof structure a deeper meaning beyond their practical identities.

Poverty, even if not of Necessity

One particular case is the open roof structure which, based upon antique precedents, exists from the early medieval period throughout the entirety of Western culture. Open roof structures may at first have been generated through entirely practical and economic considerations, since they obviated the need for additional flat ceilings. Since the early Middle Ages, however, certain open roof structures were left visible for reasons that had nothing to do with economics. In such cases, it is obvious that the size of the spaces spanned was not determinate, and that these kind of open structures exist in equal measure in secular and sacred buildings. They all share the quality that they rise above a space that is conceived and configured as a single unified space. Thus, behind open roof structure lies an aesthetic intention with regard to spatial configuration which is typical of certain times and certain buildings.

It is noticeable that the art historical research has hardly taken notice of this phenomenon. Common ideas about the teleological evolution of art, which develops over centuries from simple to complex and from old-fashioned to progressive are hardly suited to train attention onto the open roof structure. Timber building in itself enjoys a much lower prestige in terms of research than does stone building, with the exception of special research into timber construction. In the scholarly literature on medieval architecture, spaces with open roof structures are often connoted as retrograde compared to vaulted spaces or, as is the case in the research on the churches of the Franciscan order whose building codes prohibited vaulting the nave, are accepted as typical, if not

God-given.[2] This prohibition (not always observed) corresponded to the building sensibility of the beggars' order, which is characterized by the ideals of poverty, modesty and stringency.

One of the large Franciscan churches is Santa Croce, Florence (begun in 1294–1995). With its 90-meter-long and almost 20-meter-wide central nave, it is among the largest interior spaces in Christian architecture as a whole, and thus approaches the late Antique Basilica of St Peter in Rome (first quarter of the 4th century). Despite its enormous dimension and impressive appearance, it celebrates the Franciscan ideal of poverty by means of its parsimonious and stringent forms. The open roof structure recalls metaphorically the simplicity of a simple dwelling, perhaps even the stall in which Christ was born, or a barn. "Preaching barns" was the name given to the churches built by the order. The slow rhythm of arcades and the strict articulation of the wall up to the roof's springing point make the nave of Santa Croce a tectonically profiled, legible space. The fact that it is perceived as an expansive "single room" is above all attributable to the open roof structure, whose joining beams bind the space into narrow rows and, at the same time, allow the gaze up to the kingposts and the slope of the purlin courses. The fact that the important art historian Werner Gross, in a text on Santa Croce, speaks about a "flat roofing" might illustrate how often the essence of the open roof structure is overlooked – not everything that is not vaulted is flat![3]

The Aftermath of Antique Precedents

It is not certain that the Church of Old St Peters, mentioned above, and the early Christian Lateran basilica in Rome actually had open timber framed roof structures, as later representations show. In any case, these early Christian basilicas determined the church type with simple, open-roof structures well into the Middle Ages and beyond. The closest to these precedents in temporal terms as well is Sant'Apollinare in Classe in Ravenna (dedicated in 549). It offers the contemporary visitor the purest impression of an early Christian basilica. A stunning example of an open timber-framed roof structure can also be found in the Cathedral of Monreale (1174–1189). The King of Sicily, William II, had it erected from 1176 to 1189 in connection with a ruler's palace. As a representative sacred building after the precedent of the Roman Lateran, the church incorporated explicit claims to power. Despite the short distance to the seat of the bishopric of Palermo, Monreale was elevated to the status of an Archbishopric in 1183. The basilica was furnished with Antique columns and decorated with mosaics of which the most important, in the primary apse, shows Pantocrator. At his feet are the thrones of the king to the left and the bishop to the right. The space's strong coloration is framed by the equally colorfully painted beams of the roof structure.[4] It has little to do with the later open roof structures of the Franciscan churches. It is important to note a particular element: between the joining beams, along the kingpost, are regular rows of golden, "small wooden domes."[5] Whether these are really only opulent decoration will be considered further below.

In addition to a few extravagant examples such as Monreale, Cefalù or Messina, there are many Italian churches from the (early) Romanesque period which use this type of simply constructed open roof structure, among them the cathedral in Torcello (1008), San Miniato al Monte in Florence (1070–1093, clerestory and roof 1128–1150) as well as a series of small parish churches in Tuscany and Umbria. In Switzerland, one also finds this type, particularly in Ticino.[6] In the poorer areas, the roof structure was certainly left open for economic reasons; this is true for buildings from the 11th century through those of the 18th. It remains to note that even in the 19th century, several significant churches which expressly sought a connection to early Christian basilica used the simply constructed open roof structure not only as a quotation but also to refer to the origins of the Christian faith. Noteworthy here are St Boniface – the so-called "old basilica" in Munich (1834–1837, dedicated in 1850) by Georg Friedrich Ziebland – the Friedenskirche in Potsdam (1845–1848) by Ludwig Persius and August Stüler as well as

Santa Croce, Florence, 1294/95 to 1385.

Sant'Apollinare in Classe, Ravenna, dedicated 549.

Cathedral of Monreale, 1174–1189.

Cathedral of Torcello, dedicated 1008.

the Liebfrauen Church in Zurich, Switzerland, by August Hardegger (1893–1894).

The Roof as the Heavens

Another layer of meaning accruing to the open roof construction in medieval churches is the least obvious. A sideways glance at small pieces of architecture can, however, offer a basis for understanding. As early as the late antique period, so-called gable sarcophagi are known to have existed, carved from porphyry if they were meant to serve as tombs for important people.

One such tomb from the mid 5th century has been preserved in Istanbul's Hagia Eirene.[7] The house form (as dwelling for the dead) could not be clearer in appearance: a rectangular box with a roof lid. The cross with Christian monogram in the gable field is characteristic. This divides the two portions of the sarcophagus into zones, a lower one which held the body and an upper one, dedicated to the divinity and the heavenly spheres. Unimportant for the unequivocal definition of the symbolic level is whether the interior of the roof structure is open. The house form as dwelling and amplification of the person who lies within or beneath it was a given type since early Christianity. It was used for sarcophagi or grave markers and for smaller vessels such as reliquaries to represent the relationship between below and above, earth and heaven, mortal man and immortal divinity, the here and the transcendental.

In the Cathedral of Palermo, there is a row of gravestones from the Norman rulers and the Staufers who followed them. One particularly impressive burial area numbers four sarcophagi, among them that of the most important family member, Friedrich II, German-Roman Emperor. The sarcophagus of his father, Heinrich IV, his mother Constanza von Hohenstaufen and his grandfather Roger II are all in the immediate vicinity. It is significant relative to our topic that the sarcophagi are each located in small aedicules which, aside from small differences in ornament, are very similarly built: six columns upon a base carry an architrave above which a simple gabled roof rises and – their structures are open. Typologically

August Hardegger, Liebfrauenkirche, Zurich, 1893/94.

Porphyry sarcophagus, middle of the 5th Century, Hagia Eirene, Istanbul.

and formally, the aedicules follow the precedent of the antique temple and thus point
to the claim to power of a new Roman
emperor. Even for the tomb of a ruler, this
extremely explicit connection is extraordinary and, it seems, Antique precedents from
the city of Rome were directly at play.[8] In
the case of this tomb, worldly claims are
connected to medieval religious symbolism
which could not develop the desired effect
without the open roof structure. The imperi-
al stone sarcophagus which rests upon the
aedicule incorporates – turned towards the
open roof structure – figural medallions with
representations of Jesus Christ, Mary and
the four Evangelists. The burial aedicules,
essentially baldachins in conformity with,
and incorporating accepted status symbols,
again reveal below and above, the transitory
and the constant heaven in which God,
Maria and the Word of God dwell. The open
roof structure opens the two spheres to each
other, recommends the deceased to the
heavens and puts him under the protection
of divine mercy in the concrete and metaphorical sense. Essentially, the open roof
structure embodies the most originary form
of the protective and communicative baldachin. This is also true for the open timber
roof structure of the medieval church. The
earthly region of the church space is seamlessly connected to the heavenly.

Now we can reconsider Monreale, in
which the roof beams are hung with those
curious wooden domes: they are wooden
baldachins or canopies, which embody
the roof structure as baldachin and heaven
in a doubly meaningful form.

The Space of the Heavens

For the interpretation of the roof as open
heavens, we can also make reference to pro-
fane buildings. The art of medieval carpen-
try achieved particular virtuosity in England.
Countless parish churches there have open
roof structures. Unlike mainland Europe, England developed freely spanning truss-like
structures in addition to the typical roof constructions: the hammer-beam roofs. These
permitted the spanning of great dimensions.

In the later Middle Ages, each ruling
power's complex of buildings included a hall,
which is typologically derived from the
abbey refractory, but which gains increasing
independence and finally becomes synony-
mous with the ruling power's status.[9] More
than a few of these halls in England are
spanned by hammer-beam roofs which, by
their nature, are open roof structures.[10] The
largest and most famous hammer-beam roof
hall still in existence is Westminster Hall in
London, built from 1394–1402. The master
carpenter Hugh Herland is responsible for
the roof construction. Its dimensions are
staggering: the space is 73 meters long, and
the hammer beam roof spans 21 meters and
weighs nearly 660 tons![11] For more specific
information on this complex construction,
about which there is still much to say, there
is recourse to special literature.[12] The lower
the center of gravity on these kinds of roofs,
the more stabile they are. For this reason,
the roof at Westminster Hall springs from a
point halfway up the wall. The form of the
hall has something sacral about it although
it was used for secular purposes. Rib-like
timber girts span, as in a vaulted church,
up to the first horizontal collar beams. At
the spandrel of the overlapping beams are
wooden chords which contribute to the shear
reinforcement of the construction. The larger than life-size statues in the thirteen wall
niches do not represent saints but rather
English kings. The work of the sculptor
Walter Walton, they belong among the best
products of English sculpture of the latter
14th century. The fact that the sacred atmosphere is not only conceived as a vague reference but rather as an explicit connection
is also evidenced by the figures of angels,
which populate the hammer-beam roof. The
metaphor of open roof construction as city
of heaven, is even more clear in the parish
church of Saint Wendreda in the English
city of March, where a total of 120 angels
hang in the hammer-beam ceiling.[13]

The example of Westminster Hall's open
roof structure demonstrates the way in
which the concept of church vault as heavens, common throughout the entire Middle
Ages, also extended to secular buildings.
Consequently, open roof structures were, for
a long time, part of a cosmos of ideas which
inspired art and architecture. Beyond their

Tomb of Kaiser Friedrich II in the Cathedral of Palermo.

Hugh Herland, Westminster Hall, 1394–1402, Hammer-beam Roof. Representation by Augustus Charles Pugin and Thomas Rowlandson.

Saint Wendreda in March, Cambridgeshire, 1523–1526.

functional construction and their practical applications, they were symbolic spaces which – consciously formed in this way – were meant to transcend the mundane.

1 *Handwörterbuch des deutschen Aberglaubens,* Vol. 2, Berlin/New York 1987, column 117.
2 Wolfgang Braunfels, *Abendländische Klosterbaukunst,* Cologne 1978, p. 307f. ("Aus den Statuten der Franziskaner").
3 Werner Gross, *Gotik und Spätgotik,* Frankfurt/M. 1969, p. 133.
4 The painting was restored in 1811 after a fire. (Wolfgang Krönig, *The Cathedral of Monreale and Norman Architecture in Sicily,* Palermo 1965, p. 45).
5 Krönig, *The Cathedral of Monreale and Norman Architecture in Sicily,* op.cit, p. 45.
6 For example, SS. Giovanni Evangelista e Martino in Bironico, the Chiesa Rossa at Castel San Pietro, the oratorio Santa Maria del Castello in Osogna, S. Abbondio in Mezzovico, Santa Maria in Bedano, S. Maurizio in Rovello, S. Martino in Sonvico, S. Vigilio in Rovio, SS. Pietro e Paolo in Sureggio, SS. Matteo e Maurizio in Cagiallo, S. Stefano al Colle in Miglieglia, S. Giorgio in Morbio Inferiore and others.
7 Richard Delbrueck, *Antike Porphyrwerke* (Studien zur spätantiken Kunstgeschichte 6), Berlin/Leipzig 1932, p. 223f.
8 Ingo Herklotz, "Lo spazio della morte e lo spazio della sovranità", in: Mario D'Onofrio (Ed.), *I Normanni. Popolo d'Europa 1030–1200,* Venice 1994, p. 326.
9 Günter Kowa, *Architektur der englischen Gotik,* Cologne 1990, p. 253.
10 On the development of the hammer-beam roof, see: Anthony Emery, *Dartington Hall,* Oxford 1970.
11 Otto von Simson, *Das Mittelalter II* (Propyläen Kunstgeschichte, Vol. 6), Berlin 1972, p. 165.
12 Herbert Cescinsky/Ernest R. Gribble, "Westminster Hall and Its Roof", in: *The Burlington Magazine 40,* No. 227, 1922, pp. 76–79 and 82–84. Hilary St George Saunders, *Westminster Hall,* London 1951. L.T. Courtnay, "The Westminster Hall Roof and its 14th-Century Sources", in: *Journal of the Society of Architectural Historians,* No. 43, 1984, pp. 295–309.
13 Nikolaus Pevsner, *The Buildings of England,* Cambridgeshire/Harmondsworth 1954 (2nd edition 1970), p. 437f.

Roof and Light

Roof and Light

This chapter covers the same topics as the chapter "Roof and Aperture," but from the perspective of the interior space. Whereas the problem of the aperture and its relationship to the roof plane is foregrounded in looking from the outside, it is the problem of light and its conduction that is decisive in looking from the interior; nonetheless, light is indivisibly connected to the nature of the aperture. Whether seen from outside or from the perspective of the attic space, a "hole" in the roof is more problematic than the same "hole" in a wall. In addition to the argument that the primary function of the roof – protection from climate – is undermined by a hole, it is decisive for the interior space that another kind of light enters through an aperture in the roof than through one in the wall, namely top-lighting. The two types of openings, which are most commonly found in the roof, dormers and roof windows, must be considered in this context.

Traditionally, attics are lit by means of dormers. Dormers are deformations in the roof or additive elements that bring light from the side into the attic and make it possible to use normal vertical windows, which is usually easiest to deal with in terms of construction. Using a dormer, the "hole" in the roof can be avoided, because the roof remains undisturbed in its plane, but there is no benefit from top-lighting.

Since top-lighting provides light that is much more intense than light from the side, roof apertures have the advantage over dormers that a much smaller aperture can bring greater brightness into the space. On the other hand, there is often a strong and unpleasant contrast between dark and light. Additionally, skylights, which only offer a view to the sky, are not satisfactory as the only apertures, particularly in an inhabited space, since they cannot create a relationship between interior space and its environs. Rudolf Schwarz, whom Christoph Wieser quotes in his essay, speaks quite vividly about "light that drops into these spaces from above as if into an open abyss."[1]

In the case of pitched roof surfaces, however, there are other possibilities to light a space beneath the roof. Light can thus be controlled and the light/dark contrast can be reduced inasmuch as top-lighting or even light entering from the side is conducted and reflected along the respective oblique ceiling planes. Even if the space beneath the roof is lit along its joints, in other words, using structural openings, the effect of the "hole" in the roof can be avoided.

Christoph Wieser uses two projects by the Swedish architect Klas Anshelm to describe the essential condition under which the space beneath a roof can be lit successfully: the introduction of light and aperture should not be considered separately. They are, rather, to be seen in connection with the overall space, as components of its overall effect. The two projects also demonstrate that it can be useful to separate light from view, in other words, to combine skylights for light with wall apertures for view – and thus to profit from the advantages of both kinds of apertures.

Barbara Burren

1   Rudolf Schwarz, "Wie beleuchtet man Museen?", Lecture given at the Arbeitsgemeinschaft kultureller Organisationen in Düsseldorf on 27.4.1957. Reprinted in: Wolfgang Pehnt, *Rudolf Schwarz 1897–1961. Architekt einer anderen Moderne*, Ostfildern-Ruit 1997, p. 221–225, see p. 224.

Joints at the Roof's Edge

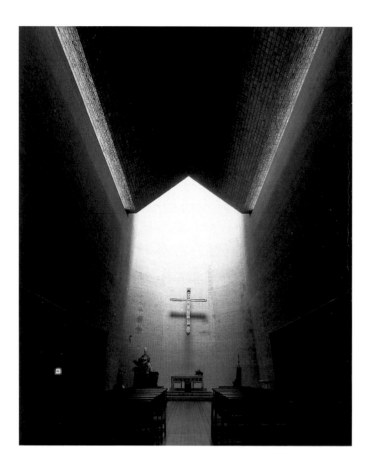

Through a joint, glancing light can be conducted into a room and thus make evident the relationship between roof and wall, or even stage that relationship dramatically. In the church of San Pedro, diffuse conduction of light along the walls gives the impression that the heavy roof is levitating while the space below the roof remains in darkness. In the Gae House in Tokyo, an unusual situation is created by the gap circumscribed between low wall and roof,

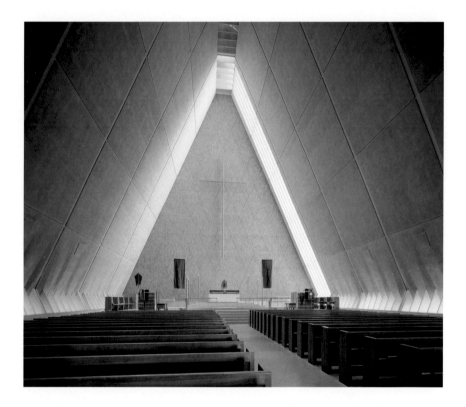

so that the light penetrates from below and moves upwards into the space, giving one the feeling of occupying a raised position. In the passenger terminal at Yokohama harbor, the brightness entering the space through a skylight is conducted continuously along pitched roof and wall surfaces to the floor, creating the impression that one is occupying a grotto-like space underground. In the Kramer chapel, on the other hand, the light beneath the roof, which extends almost to the floor, lends the religious space the character of a simple pitched tent. Light enters additionally along a single joint in the area of the choir and lights the opposing side of the roof so strongly that an almost symmetrical light situation is generated and the dark leading edge wall seems to detach itself from the roof.

Apertures punched through the roof plane create a sharp light/dark contrast between the intensive top-light and the ceiling plane, which appears dark when back-lit. Thus, in the Asama House, sunlight from a skylight in the middle of the roof strikes the opposite wall, while the space beneath the roof appears rather dark. In the living room of the house in Karui-zawa, light enters through two skylights which are directly adjacent to the gable and emphasize the height of the space beneath the roof. Reflected by a white wall, the light serves the entire room, while the large window in the façade primarily serves the view. The apertures in the school at Harby are developed across the cornice line and thus consolidate the qualities of skylight and window. They create a strong back-lit situation, but connect wall and roof and make the entire space into a "space beneath the roof" although only a narrow strip of sloped roof plane is visible.

Any perforation in a roof plane is always a wound. If this wound is, however, repeated and distributed across the roof plane, a pattern can be generated which appears to be an essential quality of the roof and not a disturbance in it. With an increasing number of openings, the light entering a building becomes more even which also amplifies the effect of the entire space beneath the roof. If the perforations are placed as closely as they are in the roof of the Boots factory, the penetrating, intensive light seems to dissolve the roof into a translucent membrane. The transition from a perforated to a translucent roof is fluid. Thus, it is the viewer's judgment which determines whether the roof of the therapy room in the rehab clinic in Basel is perforated or translucent.

Translucence

By means of a translucent roof, a regular distribution of light is achieved, although the quality of that light is decisively influenced by the density and dimension of the roof structure. In the Multi-hall in Mannheim and the Pavilion Nouvelle DestiNation at the Expo.02, the light is quite intensive; in addition, the hull structure of the Expo Pavilion is so fine and dense that it is hardly perceived, creating a strangely diffuse, almost foggy spatial impression. By means of the flat, weft-like roof construction of the children's daycare center in Odate, direct sunlight enters and creates the roof pattern on the floor, whereas it is so strongly diffused by the deep, fin-like roof beams of the Otaniemi auditorium that the space is lit by regular, indirect light.

Frei Otto **Multi-hall, Mannheim, 1972**
e2a Eckert Eckert **Pavilion Nouvelle DestiNation, Expo.02, Biel, 2002**
Shigeru Ban **Children's Daycare Center, Imai Hospital, Odate, 2001**
Alvar Aalto **Auditorium, Technical College of Otaniemi, 1964**

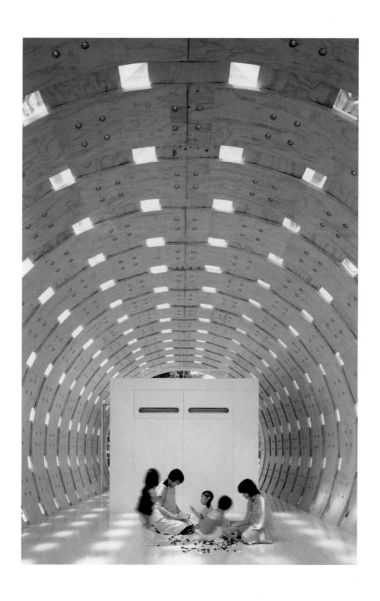

Unlike the perforation, the joint is not a wound in the roof, but rather a gap between its structural members. It brings light into the space and can at the same time contribute to a better understanding of the roof. The only opening at the apogee of the Pantheon emphasizes the centrality and introversion of the space. The light entering is so diffusely spread that it is able, surprisingly, to light the enormous space. In the TWA terminal in New York, the joints divide the roof in segments and lend it the weightlessness of outstretched wings, whereas in the Church in Hüttwilen, the joint can only be perceived by virtue of the reflection along the ceiling and wall surfaces of the light entering. In the image of the warehouse in Juanico, the joints in the roof are also invisible but their construction can be precisely read by means of the reflection of light on the arced roof elements. By means of the repetition of joints, as is typical of a shed roof, it is possible to achieve a regular, directional lighting within the entire space.

Spaces of Light

A roof dormer of any form or a raised light vessel can introduce sidelight into the space beneath the roof. An oval dormer in the Möller House in Zermützel appears to be part of the space as a whole because of its special location in the high façade, whereas in the case of the classical roof dormer in the Beckenhof Housing Project, a separate space of light is created by the direct sidelight and its reflection on the walls and ceiling. In the Mattenhof schoolhouse, a protrusion in the roof becomes a light vessel in which light entering from an aperture (not visible in the image) is reflected and distributed through the classroom, while an aperture in the wall serves primarily for the view. In the Kiasma Museum of Art, a traditional roof dormer is reinterpreted: set into the ceiling, it brings top-light into the museum space.

Lux Guyer **Beckenhof Housing Project, Zurich, 1929**
Hans Scharoun **Möller House, Zermützel, 1938**
B.E.R.G. Architekten **Mattenhof Schoolhouse, Zurich, 2003**
Steven Holl **Kiasma Museum of Art, Helsinki, 1998**

Skylight Lanterns
Klas Anshelms Art Exhibition Halls in Lund and Malmö
Christoph Wieser

Klas Anshelm is a master of the skylight. There is hardly a building in which the Swedish architect[1] has not, in some form, conducted daylight into the spaces by means of a roof, usually sloped. Often, as is the case in both of his art exhibition spaces in Lund and Malmö, the skylights are used as elements with which to determine form and atmosphere. Anshelm loved the functional and the simple in this undertaking. That is why the incoming light is not theatrically exalted, as it often is, for example, in church buildings,[2] but rather simply used as a welcome source of daylight above all. Clarity, not transfiguration, is Anshelm's intention in the way he uses natural light, a good quality of light for the interior spaces.

To compare his approach to the principles of industrial building is even more appropriate since Anshelm was designing factory buildings which are comparable to both these art exhibition spaces. In the factories, shed roofs are generally known to have been used to light work places optimally in the simplest possible way, in other words, with northern light which is the most even and color-neutral.[3] And nonetheless, Anshelm by no means created neutrally lit spaces. Rather, he implemented light and space in his buildings precisely but in an extremely willful manner. Their strength derives less from dramatic effects than from a powerful physical presence, evoked by the raw, almost coarse-seeming materialization and the differentiated use of daylight. His buildings are, in the best way, pragmatic but also uncomfortable in their radicalism. They emanate a realism which recalls Ingmar Bergman specifically in the sense that his films deal with reality: mercilessly, directly, but with a high level of artistic ambition. This is expressed in the masterful use of light which seems natural but not naturalistic, since it purposively emphasizes or deemphasizes the things that support the plot, using soft or contrasting plays of light.

The comparison with Bergman is also interesting because he subverts the individual to speak to the mood of an era. In the second half of the 1950s, museum building experienced a paradigm shift. There was a demand for a move away from the sky-lit galleries of the 19th century with their natural light and a reorientation towards direct side-lighting.[4] 1957 was the year in which Bergman's revolutionary films *Wild Strawberries* and *The Seventh Seal* came to theaters and Anshelm opened his first important building, the exhibition hall in Lund. It was the same year that saw the opening of Rudolf Schwarz and Josef Bernard's Wallraf Richartz Museum in Cologne, the first German museum of the post-war period. Against this background, Schwarz held a lecture entitled "Wie beleuchtet man Museen?" (How does one light museums?),[5] in which the new attitude was expressed. A museum should be a well-lit house, "flooded with real light from the rising and setting of the sun and its midday brightness, open to the landscape as it revitalizes itself in the sky and the organic world. […] The best means by which to show [works of art] in their best light is the simple window, which lets light in without artifice and unchanged, and not the indirect, filtered light that drops into these spaces from above as if into an open abyss."[6] Schwarz could only realize this desire in part, since the direction for the presentation of the collection demanded a high proportion of classical top-lit spaces.[7]

Lund Exhibition Hall 1954–1957

The exhibition hall in Lund is, relative to daylighting, a transitional work. Anshelm combined unfiltered side lighting with a diffusely spread top lighting, which is in itself not unusual. The way in which the apertures are made, however, the choice of materials and the atmosphere created make the building decidedly different from traditional museums. Anshelm himself compared the building in his own, dry manner with its predecessors: "The exhibition hall in Lund with its excellent location on Mårtenstorget replaced a butcher's shop. This shop was in its own way a relatively attractive exhibition space. In art exhibition spaces, as is known, pictures of painted hares and chickens are shown. In this space, dead hares and chickens were shown. There were skylights. Quite a beautiful complex."[8]

One enters the building, oriented along the northerly plaza end of Mårtenstorget,

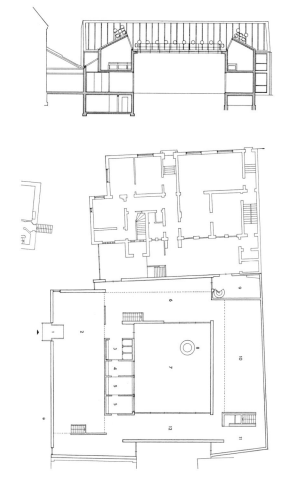

Exhibition hall, Lund; view towards the
ringing gallery in the upper storey.

Exhibition hall, Lund; primary facade with
the entrance on Märtenstorget.

Exhibition hall, Lund; section and plan.

Exhibition hall, Lund, with staircase to gallery.

Ehibition hall, Lund, original lighting
using spotlights in the courtyard.

through a small windbreak, and stands
immediately within a two-storey exhibition
space that is brightly lit by means of an
oblique skylight which spans the entire
width of the space. Along both lateral sides
on the ground floor are adjacent spaces,
narrow and attenuated, which are lit by
means of a central courtyard. They lead to
the second hall at the rear portion of the
site. The gallery level wraps the courtyard
and conjoins the halls by means of an ambu-
latory. All spaces in the upper storey receive
a large amount of daylight through shed
roof-like apertures. Of these apertures, however, only the one in the largest hall is oriented to the north. The others orient themselves towards the internal courtyard, which
centers the complex and makes of the exhibition hall something of a sundial: all its
spaces receive direct sunlight over the
course of the day.

For this period, it was an entirely new
lighting concept, and it corresponds to the
unusual use of materials and color. The
floor is made of grey stone pavers or black
linoleum, the walls are clad with jute and
painted light or dark grey, the ceilings in the
ground floor level are covered in mineral-
bound wood wool boards and the underside
of the raw concrete roof is painted.[9] These
raw, light-absorptive surfaces were complimented by the greenish wire glass[10] used for
the skylights – a material that has been
widespread for many years in the skylights
of industrial buildings.[11] Its irregular, lightly
rippled surface broke the light entering –
there is no protection against the sun – and
acted like a "sifter" to distribute and soften
the light. In combination with the strongly
absorptive surfaces, this created a gently
lit atmosphere with soft shadows, as can be
recognized in contemporary photographs.
One interesting detail connected to this
effect is the nature of electric light in the
exhibition spaces. In order to obviate the
need for direct artificial light in the evenings
or under poor weather conditions, Anshelm
installed numerous floodlights on the balustrade of the interior courtyard; they light
the interior spaces through the glass.[12]

As a counterpoint to the wire glass-filled
skylight lanterns, Anshelm used clear glass

for the other windows, so that direct sunlight entered the room at these points to create a clear, contoured formation of light and shadow. The mild light is dominant, however, and is reinforced by the position of the windows and by the shape of the roof. Nearly all apertures are defined as gaps, as narrow bands of large structural openings. Because they are pushed to the edge of a wall or occupy an entire field in the wall, and because the skylights are formed as shed roofs fully glazed on one side, the light is conducted and reflected deep into the spaces along the adjacent wall or ceiling planes.

The principle of the partially opened, often oblique roof plane is one that Anshelm studied in countless variations in his work, be it in the lucarnes of his office and apartment building in Lund, a renovation and addition that he completed bit by bit between 1955 and 1969; in the skylights, also triangular-shaped, of the Botanical Physiological Institute at the University of Lund (1961); or in the complexly composed roofscape, made up of shed and pitched roofs, of the cafeteria building for the adult education center in Fridhem (1965). By means of incising and unfolding, or by shifting roof planes against one another, he achieved formally interesting roof forms and pleasing interior lighting using simple means. Just how pragmatically he worked on this problem is demonstrated exemplarily in the Lund exhibition hall: because the two large halls are higher than the gallery that connects them, there is an overlap of the shed roof geometry at the corners. Anshelm "solves" this problem by allowing the lower roofs simple to puncture the glass planes of the higher spaces, which leads to somewhat crude detailing. By doing so, however, he achieves a situation in which the roof planes seem heavy since the thickness of the concrete slabs is legible and the effect of gravity visible as it pulls against the unfolded planes.

Exhibition Hall in Malmö 1971–1973

If the exhibition hall in Lund recalls a "spiritualized factory,"[13] then there is also something factory or workshop-like about the exhibition hall in Malmö[14], Anshelm's last great building. Its geometry is closely

Klas Anshlem, Botanical physiological Institute in Lund.

Klas Anshelm's office in his own house on Kävlingevägen in Lund.

associated with that of the machine assembly hall for the construction machinery factory Landsverk AG in Landskrona,[15] built by Anshelm in 1951. Both are large-scale halls whose silhouettes are dominated by one singular prismatic skylight which sits on them slightly asymmetrically. Even the cladding of the skylights with sheet aluminum is done at Malmö exactly as it was in the industrial building twenty years before. This is typical of Anshelm, who worked up a repertoire of constructional and formal solutions over the course of time, which he used again and again.[16] In Landskrona, the skylight is placed so that the offices, which are adjacent to the assembly hall beneath the slightly sloped roof also receive daylight, a sectional solution that is as elegant as it is efficient.

In terms of its character, the exhibition hall in Malmö is meant to recall a workshop.[17] For that reason, the 30 x 75 meter area is entirely undivided, except for the zoning created by the large skylight lantern.[18] Even the materialization is an invitation to change the building with every new exhibition. Thus, the floor is made of planed spruce boards in which the nails are visible, and the walls were clad in untreated fire protection panels made of extruded mica (Vermit).[19] The atmosphere of an open workshop corresponds to Anshelm's vision of architecture as something functional, vital and adaptable, but it is also in agreement with the demand of that era to democratize the once temple-like museum.[20]

As in Lund, the apertures in Malmö are also structural in nature, and here, too, the light atmosphere on the interior is essentially determined by the roof windows. Next to the shed skylight already mentioned, which opens the rather low 3.5-meter high space to the sky at a height of 10 meters along two-thirds of its entire length, a large portion of the remaining roof surface is perforated with hundreds of rectangular skylight lanterns. These are closely spaced, so that a blanket of light is created which falls equally in the exhibition space. And although all roof apertures are oriented to the north, the contrast between the lower portion with its small lanterns and the zone with the large skylight creates varied, lighter

and darker areas of alternating light quality which give the room an introverted sense in some areas and a definitively extroverted one in another. Unlike his work in Lund, here Anshelm uses clear glass everywhere, so that the sky is present in the building. Through the large skylight, one also sees the crowns of the trees to which the plan consciously defers.

The building does have a flat roof, but the roof is formed as a space-containing landscape: each of the 528 skylight lanterns[21] is configured as an asymmetrical, funnel-like opening with a view to the sky. The slightly curved plywood panels in the lower area are complimented by an encircling aluminum frame into which the two sockets for simple light bulbs are routed; the whole is closed by a frameless, adhesive-applied insulated glass panel.[22] In detail, these elements seems somewhat "tinkered", which reflects not only the pressures of cost but also Anshelm's search for simple solutions. His predilection for rawness and for the unconventional use of inexpensive materials was something he shared with Sigurd Lewerentz, whose atelier in the garden of his own house Anshelm built: a wooden box without windows, clad on the interior and exterior with roof paper and provided with daylight only by means of three skylight lanterns.

The idea to build a roof out of a series of light catchers was first developed by Anshelm in his 1958 competition for the Nordic pavilion at the Venice Biennale,[23] which was ultimately realized by Sverre Fehn. There is one well-known – at least in Scandinavia – precedent: the Swedish pavilion for the 1937 World's Fair in Paris by Sven Ivar Lind.[24] In this building, Lind had lighted part of the pavilion used as an exhibition hall with closely spaced square roof windows.[25] Unlike Anshelm, he concealed the full height of the construction behind a suspended milk glass pane.[26] The materials were similarly raw and tough: the walls and ceiling of the red steel construction were clad in mineral-bound wood wool panels (Heraklit) onto which the works exhibited were directly mounted. The floor was covered with linoleum and the underside of the intermediate floorslab was prefabricated, exposed concrete.[27]

Exhibition hall, Malmö

View on approach with
the large skylight lantern.

In the divisible exhibition hall the skylights
structure the room.

Lateral section and ground floor plan.

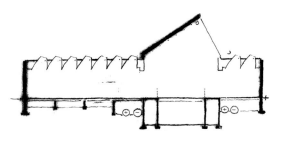

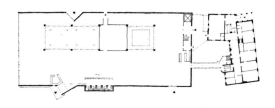

Exhibition hall, Malmö, roofscape.

The two cultural buildings in Lund and Malmö mark an important milestone in Anshelm's long and successful career: if the exhibition hall in Lund represented his success in achieving recognition as an independent architect, then the exhibition hall in Malmö seems to be the quintessence of his work. An individualist like Lewerentz, he pursued only a few ideas doggedly and consistently. Among those were a preference for raw materials as well as the search for ever-new and surprising solutions for pitched roofs in combination with skylights.

1   There is little literature on Klas Anshelm (1914–1980). The most comprehensive (Swedish) literature is by Per Qvarnström: Per Qvarnström, *Arkitekt Klas Anshelm, samlade arbeten*, Stockholm 1998. In addition to various descriptions of buildings in the Swedish journal *Byggmästaren* and later in *Arkitektur*, the journal *Arkitektur* published a monographic issue on Anshelm in July, 1979. There is a slim volume available in English: Olof Hultin (Ed.), *The Architecture of Klas Anshelm*, Stockholm 2004. In German, to my knowledge, there is only my review of the Swedish-English publication by Olof Hultin mentioned above: Christoph Wieser, "Klas Anshelm? Klas Anshelm!", in: *werk, bauen + wohnen*, No. 10, 2004, p. 62 f.

2   These "skylight spotlights" are well known; they project light directly on an altar or statue and pull it dramatically from the semi-darkness. Le Corbusier used the appropriate term for these "canons à lumiere", for example, when describing the skylights above the side chapels at the Convent of La Tourette.

3   Fritz Hefele, *Das Fabrik-Oberlicht*, Berlin 1931, p. 2.

4   Hannelore Schubert, *Moderner Museumsbau. Deutschland Österreich Schweiz*, Stuttgart 1986, p. 9.

5   Rudolf Schwarz, "Wie beleuchtet man Museen?", Lecture given at the Arbeitsgemeinschaft kultureller Organisationen in Düsseldorf on 27. 4. 1957. Reprinted in: Wolfgang Pehnt, *Rudolf Schwarz 1897–1961. Architekt einer anderen Moderne*, Ostfildern-Ruit 1997, p. 221–225.

6   Ibid., p. 224.

7   Schubert, *Moderner Museumsbau. Deutschland Österreich Schweiz*, op.cit., p. 9.

8   Qvarnström, *Arkitekt Klas Anshelm, samlade arbeten*, op. cit., p. 110.

9   Klas Anshelm, "Konsthall i Lund", in: Byggmästaren, No. 1 1958, pp. 18–23; and: Qvarnström, *Arkitekt Klas Anshelm, samlade arbeten*, op. cit., pp. 110–115. Today the walls are painted white, giving the space a much harsher atmosphere.

10 According to a telephone conversation between the author and Per Qvarnström on 15. 8. 2007. In *Byggmästaren* the glass is called "raw glass". See: Anshelm, "Konsthall i Lund", op. cit., p. 19.

11 Hefele, *Das Fabrik-Oberlicht*, op. cit., p. 19.

12 Anshelm "Konsthall i Lund", as above, p. 23. The only trace remaining is the balustrade in the courtyard. The lights have been dismounted and replaced by spots on the interior which are pointed towards the ceiling.

13 A "spiritualized factory" is what the central Swiss painter Hans von Matt wanted for his new studio, built for him by Armin Meili in 1927 in Stans. He meant "a place of work which expresses the function of its designation and at the same time should represent the many sides of its occupant," as Hilar Stadler writes. See: Hilar Stadler, "Demonstrationsstücke im Banngebiet des Schweizerischen Heimatschutzes. Atelierhäuser der Moderne im Raum Zentralschweiz", in: *Kunst + Architektur*, No. 3, 2002, p. 50.

14 For the exhibition hall in Malmö see: *Arkitektur*, No. 3, 1977, p. 12–19; and: Qvarnström, *Arkitekt Klas Anshelm, samlade arbeten*, op. cit., p. 232–239.

15 See Klas Anshelm, "Montageverksad i Landskrona", in: Byggmästaren, No. 31, 1956, p. 34 f.; and: Qvarnström, *Arkitekt Klas Anshelm, samlade arbeten*, op. cit., p. 70–77.

16 For example, in Malmö Anshelm had also mounted floodlights outside the large skylights for the nightime lighting of the interior space.

17 Klas Anshelm, "Malmö konsthall", in: *Arkitektur*, No. 3, 1977, p. 12.

18 Originally, there was a small separate lecture hall beneath one of the four parts of the large skylight. See: Qvarnström, *Arkitekt Klas Anshelm, samlade arbeten*, op. cit., p. 238.

19 Jan Torsten Ahlstrand, "Malmö konsthall: en öppen arkitektur?", in: *Arkitektur*, No. 3, 1977, p. 17.

20 Schubert, *Moderner Museumsbau. Deutschland Österreich Schweiz*, op. cit., p. 13.

21 Qvarnström, *Arkitekt Klas Anshelm, samlade arbeten*, op. cit., p. 234.

22 According to a telephone conversation between the author and Per Qvarnström on 15. 8. 2007.

23 Qvarnström, *Arkitekt Klas Anshelm, samlade arbeten*, op. cit., p. 236.

24 For the architecture of Sven Ivar Lind see:Tomas Lewan, "Sven Ivar Lind. Arkitekt och pedagog", in: *Arkitektur*, No. 4, 1994, p. 4–32; and: Christoph Wieser, "Poesie und Abstraktion", in: *werk, bauen und wohnen*, No. 6, 2002, p. 60–64.

25 "Sveriges Paviljong på Parisutställningen", in: *Byggmästaren*, No. 31, 1937, pp. 339–366.

26 A comparison of Lind's and Anshelm's sections at the skylights can be found in: Lewan, "Sven Ivar Lind. Arkitekt och pedagog", op. cit., p. 7.

27 See ibid., and: Wieser, "Poesie und Abstraktion", op. cit.

Tetto gigantesco – a different big roof

The new headquarters of the Società Ippica Torinese (S.I.T.) in Nichelino/Torino, 1958/59,
by Gabetti e Isola, Architetti, and Giuseppe Raineri, Ingegnere

Aita Flury

"Just as the interior space in which one must live, becomes the building's reality, the emphasis on shelter, on the sheltering roof, becomes more meaningful in character and more important an element than ever before."
Frank Lloyd Wright[1]

The story of Gabetti e Isola Architetti is a story of big roofs. Even if the description of their work relative to the singular, continual progressive development of one topic does not do justice to their uninterrupted power of innovation, it is evident that one of their essential studies dealt with the essence and potential of enormous sloped roofs. This is proven by numerous examples of their public buildings: the early Palazzo della Borsa Valori Torino (1952/53), the late parish hall in Bagnolo (1975–1980) or the paradigmatic Casa Pero in Pino Torinese (1965–1968), exemplary for housing of all scales. Decisive for all roofs is the formulation of the hip, which is elevated through unusual incisions and composition to a geometrically folded planar roofscape. These are enormous roofs, which, as expanding, space-forming constructs create a sheltering conclusion to and intersection with the sky; they have become the overarching insignia of Gabetti e Isola Architetti.

The Development of an Idea

The idea of the roof as sculptural modulator is metonymous for the general search for identity within the *doppoguerra*,[2] which would lead to a new poetic realism of place and concrete presence. In the romantic counter-reaction to Modernism, which was seen as too emotionless, the pitched roof was rediscovered as the form-defining means. Within the new consciousness of history and tradition, and within the intellectual logic of the 1950s, no other building component lent itself as well to giving a building character and expression. Roof forms, understood as multivalent total, thus became independent aesthetic values. Nonetheless, they are distant from later, simplistic reductions to the iconic. The rediscovery of the roof as expressive fifth façade leads in fact to a new relationship between the building volume's

formation, the definition of internal space and construction: with the liberation of the section from its self-imposed paralysis by the "horizontal idea" of Modernism, the possibilities of different height spaces and of allowing the roof to be sensed immediately within the building are demonstrated with renewed vigor.

In their efforts to unify emotional aspects and rational moments, Gabetti e Isola overlay the aesthetic will to form with a search for economic and structural efficiency in the case of the roof. The development of the structure, most often in collaboration with the structural engineer Giuseppe Raineri, demonstrates their closeness to Italy's structural experimentalism of the period. Compared to Riccardo Morandi or Luigi Nervi's shell structures, what is at stake here is an ingenious structural empiricism, whose interest owes less to the "pure form" than to the crafts-based logic of the construction site amidst the technical probing of the era's conventional building methods. Structural blurriness is taken as an opportunity to intensify the specificity and pictorial density of roof form and space. One impressive example of this quality is the riding school building for the Società Ippica Torinese (S.I.T.) in Nichelino, a suburb of Torino.

Sheltering Roof

The first reference for the new headquarters of the S.I.T. was the Cavalleriza[3] in the Corso Massimo d'Azegli in Torino, built between 1937 and 1940 by Carlo Mollino. This early project of the great Torino master had to give way to a new high school because of its inner-city site, and Gabetti e Isola were asked to design a replacement for it. In an initially site-less project development phase, their first, relatively well resolved designs depict an expanded layout which references Mollino's modernist subdivision of functions into individual volumes. From the beginning, however, a centralizing hip-shaped roof/hat with an extremely attenuated center monumentalizes and counteracts the functional order.[4] It is only in the later design phases, and concretely, in the projects related to the available site in Nichelino, that the decisive typological shift

Arial view: From this perspective, the roof form appears
textile and soft.

View from northwest.

occurs: all horse and hay stalls as well as the primary and secondary spaces for the riders are pulled together and attached to the centrally built volume of the riding hall. Ostensibly, this tautened organization builds upon energy and economic parameters. Primarily, however, it is the expression of an architecturally superordinate interest in a *forma chiusa,* a closed form as the rigid basic order, and its contrast to a "serrated" roof. The densification of the buildings to a compact monoblock makes it possible for the rooms and functions to be collected in direct adjacency to one another under *one* roof. The fascination lies in the gigantic roof that conjoins everything: a bent continuum of surface which comprises a number of singular, sloped planes conjoined to form a tent-like fabric of impressive dimensions.

Aerial photography facilitates the framing of this essential images of the S.I.T. Like a piece of fabric barely raised from the ground, or like a kite, the roof "tarp" stands on delicate columns, seemingly hollow blades of grass, and seems to float. With the elegance and levity of an autumn leaf which has fallen on the ground, the roof form seems textile and soft from this perspective; the bends appear no more than the trace of a prior fold. In its ambivalence between a roof that only brushes the terrain and a constructed mass which rises from the ground, the isolated object of the S.I.T. develops an imaginative power against the relentless horizontality of the Padan landscape: a shading device or a temporary measure taken relative to the atmosphere as the originary image of the archaic need for shelter and comfort. "What else gives an old barn its interest except its enormous roof – a cliff of grey shingles exposed to the elements like a hill, its breadth emanating security and stability," wrote John Burroughs in 1914.[5] Of central significance for the topic of *shelter is* the primacy of the roof seen from any viewpoint. The force of the downwards-sloping, deeply cantilevered roof is also dominant for the sensation of the viewer on the ground and evokes in a strange way the simultaneously biomorphic and futuristic image of an enormous organism in motion.

Roof plan: Folded surface continuum.

First floor plan: Area above the horse stalls, rooms
for the club members on the western side, riding hall
in the middle.

Ground floor plan: Portico, horse stalls, riding hall.

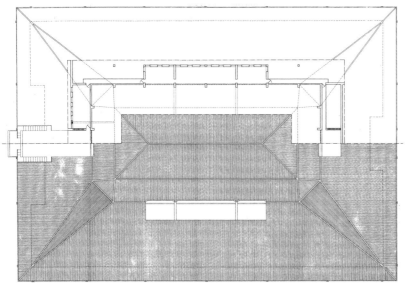

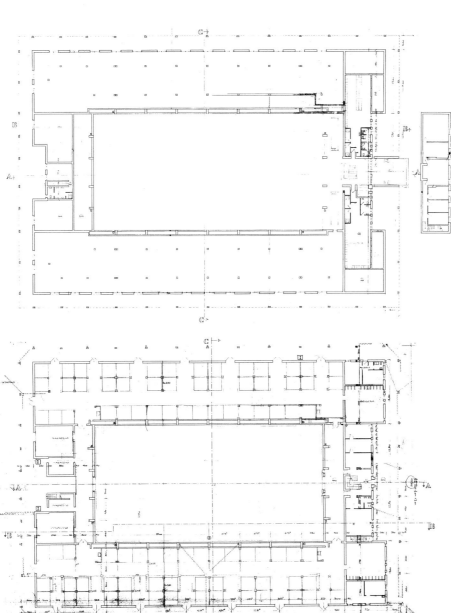

North façade: Hip-shaped roof/hat.

Longitudinal section: Overall continuity and
specific heights of respective spaces.

Airy, vertical spaces above the horse stalls.

Transitional space between interior and exterior
as accessible involution.

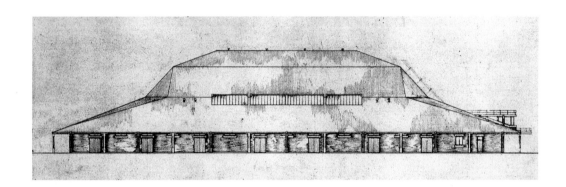

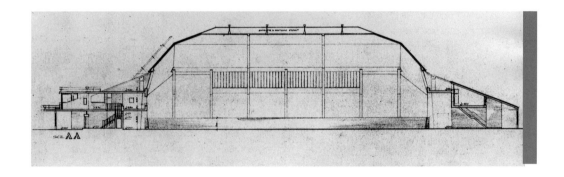

The riding hall – view to the members' rooms.

Synthesis of the Functions

On its interior, the building of the S.I.T. unifies in a unique way the overarching idea of the all-encompassing continuity of the roof with specific room heights, an attentive conduction of daylight and a simple ventilation strategy. Given the dimensions of the riding hall – 25 x 50 meters – and an overall roof area of 60 x 84 meters, this is no small achievement.

The sections show how the form of the downwards-sloping roof is cleverly unified with the functional location of the spaces that encircle the high central riding hall: the horse stalls, aligned peripherally on the longitudinal sides, are directly accessed and lit via an exterior, ring-like portico which wraps the building. The airy, uplifting spaces of the horse stalls are compressed along the threshold to the riding hall by the introduction of a two-story interstitial layer, which serves as a hayloft on its second floor. At the highest level, this buffer zone between riding hall and stalls, running along half the length of the hall, is cut out of the roof's continuum to form a negative pocket of space. These pockets mutate into light catchers for the internalized riding hall; by virtue of their deep location, they also function as apertures for cross-ventilation while remaining sheltered from the wind. Organization, lighting and ventilation of the lateral sides follow the same principle: the primary and secondary riders' rooms located there are lit directly along the façade; the incised terraces above guarantee a balanced lighting situation in the hall that is the same on all sides. A dormer-like protrusion in the serrated roof space gives extra emphasis to the entry side. In this little cabin, at an appropriate height and with a full view of the jumping area, is the jury box.

The sectional organization unifies the idea of allowing the roof to be perceived throughout the building, achieved by accommodating all spaces in the roof itself, so to speak, with the proportional reduction of unproductive space to a minimum. The unusual roof incisions warrant particular attention in several respects. On the one hand, these occupiable concave incursions permit the Eternit-panel roof covering to be main-tained with ease, since they provide simple access to and supervision of all surfaces. On the other hand, their particular meaning lies in their roles as transitional spaces between interior and exterior. In this capacity, they draw attention to the unusual connection between the hall's long-span structure and that of the exterior ring of rooms with their shorter spans. These are ambiguous loca-tions, in which the idea of continuous fold-ing and the discrepancy between inner and outer contour are exposed by the idiosyn-cratic juncture of the hybrid structural ele-ments.

Hybrid Folds

The transition between the riding hall's kinked exterior silhouette to a more arched or even domed-seeming interior space depends upon an idiosyncratic structural concept which was developed from the start in close collaboration with the engineer Giuseppe Raneri. Raneri's concept of the structure's authentic formal contribution is obvious in the overall spatial impression of the S.I.T. The translation[6] of two excerpts from a text written together by the engineer and the architects describes the structure's essential idea: "for the central riding hall, a surface bearing system[7] seemed right as a way to realize the overall, unifying idea of the built volume. In order to circumvent the need for expensive construction costs inher-ent in pure concrete structural systems,[8] this became an opportunity to create figural and structural continuity between the bearing structure of the hall and the building's outer roof slabs. The folded plate is composed of a series of conventional roof slabs made out of hollow-gauged masonry planks. These are straight, prefabricated elements which are conjoined polygonally along only a few edges." The authors describe the system's static behavior as follows: "The reinforced non-structural top screed absorbs the hori-zontal shears of the planes. Girts between the planes absorb forces along the planes' edges whereas the membrane tensile forces are absorbed by the folded plate in its entirety. The riding hall roof is closed on its narrow sides using plates that recall the arches of a cloister. They derive their form

Combination of surface structure and trusses.

Seam between the surface structure made
of prefabricated hourdis elements.

Lateral section: The surface development of the riding hall
approximates a groin vault.

Detail Section Truss and strip buttresses –
recalls the framework and infill of tent architecture.

Optical fluctation of structure between a skeleton
and a spur wall structure within the hall.

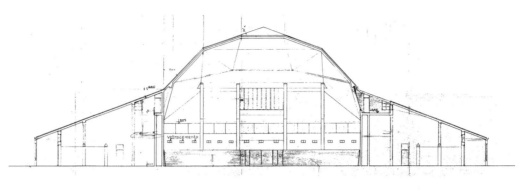

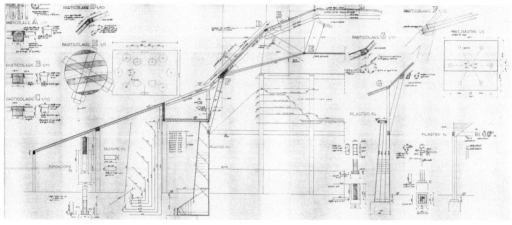

together with two truss-like girders spanning the longitudinal sides. Any excessive lateral forces deriving from the statically indeterminate pretensioning of the trusses[9] are absorbed by exterior pier buttresses which carry the building's outermost roof slabs."[10]

The system described unites two particular approaches: first, the clever and innovative idea of producing a surface structural system with the simplest means – the flat surfaces were produced inexpensively using prefabricated hollow-gauged masonry planks. This thinking speaks to the challenges of conventional, but not crafts-based, principles. Second is the unusual combination of a plate system with two trusses: a surface principle is held in place with the help of a stick system which also provides a simple means of adjustment. Plate construction types[11] are more difficult to understand than solid or framed systems; the use of a idiosyncratically overlaid system arising from the two basic decisions already discussed sets the central hall in a particularly ambivalent state of constructional ambiguity. Seen in geometric terms, the surface geometry resembles a through vault:[12] its effect is that the space appears more centered than its proportions would lead one to expect. At the same time, the spatial impression oscillates between that of a shell and that of a folded plate,[13] while the structure can be read equally as framed system or a plate construction system. The trusses and the pier buttresses recall the framework of tent architecture and lend the interior space a curious note of fragility while referencing the image of roof as light, mobile construction.

Character

The S.I.T and its roof idea do not reflect a search for the typical, but rather, for the characteristic. Its qualities derive from the idiosyncratic play of roof form, bearing structure and interior design. These all express function and fabrication, but also, the inspiration for a few precisely defined chains of association. Janus-like, the exterior image of the protective barn[14] of the S.I.T. is combined with the courtly interior of a riding hall,[15] although there, too, despite the

The riding hall – view towards the entry for horses and riders.

Hay Barn, Washington.

Christian Gottfried, Heinrich Bandhauer, Riding stable in Köthen, 1821.

richer interior design remains robust and rather raw. On the level of structure, it is the peculiarity of the ambivalent folded surface system. Unlike the idea inherent to surface constructions, that the bearing surface conforms directly to the space-defining skin, the S.I.T.'s roof is covered by a roof bonnet whose geometry is in part deviant; the configuration of the interior space is not continued. The imagistic and spatial expectations that derive from the areas of the accustomed and of constructional empiricism enter into a fruitful exchange. The S.I.T. shows off the roof paradigmatically as *the* effective means to emphasize the specific, the personal and the strange. It is finally the strange that defines the character of a building, and that makes the S.I.T. unmistakable.

Literature on Gabetti e Isola Architetti
Cellini Francesco/D'Amato Claudio, *Gabetti e Isola. Progetti e architetture 1950 – 1985,* Milan 1985.
Zermani Paolo, *Gabetti e Isola,* Bologna 1989.
Guerra Andrea/Morresi Manuela, *Gabetti e Isola.* Opere di architetture. Venice 1996.
Piva Cesare, *Gabetti & Isola. Conversazioni sull'Architettura. Il Mestiere,* Naples 2001.

1   Edgar Kaufmann and Ben Raeburn, *Frank Lloyd Wright. Schriften und Bauten,* Berlin 1997, p. 255.
2   The most evident transformation within post-war Italian architecture was the acceptance of regionalism, often on the part of converted Rationalists, but also by the protagonists of the younger generation. On the role of Gabetti e Isola during the "neoliberty" movement, see: Francesco Cellini/Claudio D'Amato, *Gabetti e Isola. Progetti e architetture 1950 – 1985,* Milan 1985, pp. 16 – 22.
3   On Carlo Mollino's S.I.T. see Armando Melis, "La Sede della Società Ippica a Torino", in: *L'architettura italiana,* February 1941, pp. 45 – 62.
4   For the design process see Andrea Guerra, *Manuela Morresi, Gabetti e Isola. Opere di architetture,* Venedig 1996, pp. 56 – 60.
5   John Burroughs, *Signs and Seasons,* New York 1914, p. 252.
6   I thank Jürg Conzett for his comprehensive support both in translating the texts from Italian and in interpreting the structural system.
7   The Italian concept "guscio" is both the general term for "surface structure" and included in the specific term "shell".
8   The advantages of the system selected are described extensively in a section of the text entitled: "Possibilità generali del sistema". They can be summarized as follows: folded plates made out of hollow-gauged masonry planks with a non-structural top screed are not much more difficult to construction than a pure (continuously curved) concrete shell; but they are stiffer and work just as well despite the faceted form. The folded plate made from flat surfaces is easier to construct than a shell and can also be enhanced along its ribs using reinforcing or cables so that it can be dimensioned for failure very economically without great deformation.
9   The truss is constructed as simply as possible; the lower cord nodes are made of drilled cylinders through which the round sections of the cord are threaded. They stick out with a cut head in such a way that the whole system can be adjusted wtih the simple turn of a nut.
10 Roberto Gabetti/Aimaro Isola/Giuseppe Raineri, *Nuova Sede Società Ippica Torinese,* Archives Gabetti e Isola.
11 On the constructional and formal basics of surface systems, see: Fred Angerer, Bauen mit tragenden Flächen. Konstruktion und Gestaltung, Munich 1960.
12 The structure is described in several publications as a "volta a padiglione" (polygonal domical vault). More precisely, it is close to a "volta a botte con testate di padiglione" (through vault). It is a conical barrel spanning a rectangular plan, which is intersected on its narrow sides by a rounded or pointed vault. See Hans Koepf/Günther Binding, *Bildwörterbuch der Architektur,* Stuttgart 1999.
13 A shell is characterized by continuous curvature, whereas a folded plate comprises individual flat plates. In itself, the transition from folded plate to shell is continuous; thus, the approximation of a shell by a folded plate is not so odd, but is still a rare case among executed examples.
14 The architects refer to the tradition of English Country Riding Clubs. These are buildings which recall rural, peripheral functional buildings and conventional wood construction; they are not expressive either of a sports facility nor do they have an industrial character. The chosen roof geometry recalls too the gambrel roofs found in the eastern US and Canada. The concept "gambrel" relates to a horse's jumping joint. The lower portion of the roof is steeply sloped while the upper portion is more gently sloped. The angle in the roof geometry permits enough headroom in the stalls and creates a space for storing hay.
15 Although the architects do not mention it, the riding hall in Köthen, 1821 von Gottfried Heinrich Bandhauer bears an astonishing similarity to the interior space. On the development of the riding hall typology, see: Liliane Skalecki. *Das Reithaus. Untersuchungen zu einer Bauaufgabe im 17. bis 19. Jh.,* Hildesheim 1992.

Authors

Max Bosshard, born 1946, 1975 graduation from the ETH Zurich. 1974 – 1976 work for Aldo Rossi, Milan, 1976 – 1982 work for Prof. Paul Hofer, Professorship for Urban History and for the design courses of Prof. Bernhard Hoesli, Prof. Paul Hofer and Prof. Aldo Rossi, ETH Zurich. 1980 – 1982 professorial assistant for Visiting Lecturer Flora Ruchat, ETHZ, 1982 – 1989 collaboration in the office of Peter Baumann, since 1990 own architectural office with Christoph Luchsinger in Lucerne. Lecturer for Design and Construction, and for Architectural and Urban Analysis at the ZHAW, since 2001 director of the Center for Urban Landscape ZHAW.

Barbara Burren, born 1962, dipl. Architect ETH SIA BSA. Studies at the ETH Zurich, graduation 1990. 1990/91 professorial assistant for Prof. Hans Kollhoff, ETH Zurich. Since 1991 independent architectural work, since 2006 with GfA Gruppe für Architektur (Group for Architecture) with Ilinca Manaila and Detlef Schulz. 1997/98 professorial assistant for Prof. Adrian Meyer, ETH Zurich. Since 1998 Lecturer for Design and Construction at the ZHAW.

Nott Caviezel, Ph. D., born 1953, art and architectural historian. 1983 – 1986 Director of the National Research Program 16, 1987 – 1995 Director of the Society for Swiss Art History, thereafter directed own research project on the late medieval church architecture of the Alpine region. Since 1985 Guest Lecturer at various universities and technical colleges. Member of the Federal Commission on Historic Preservation. Since 2002 Editor-in-Chief of the architecture journal *werk, bauen + wohnen.*

Aita Flury, born 1969, dipl. Architect ETH SIA, is Professor for Design at the CIA and the HTW in Chur. 1999 – 2001 work for Meili & Peter Architects, 2003/04 Assistant at the ETH Zurich for Staufer & Hasler Architects. Independent work as architect as well as publications on architecture, exhibitions and symposium conceptions.

Hartmut Frank, born 1942, dipl. Architect and architectural historian. Studied architecture and urban planning at the TU Berlin, teaching since 1970 at the ETHZ, TU Berlin, HfdK Hamburg among others, since 1986 at the HafenCity University Hamburg. Research and publications on the history of architecture and urban planning in the 19th and 20th centuries, exhibitions on Fritz Schumacher, Alexis de Chateauneuf, Paul Schmitthenner among others, and on the architecture of the two German states 1919–1989.

Bettina Köhler, Ph. D., born 1959, art historian. Since 2002 Professor for Art and Cultural History, since 2006 member of the board of the Institute for Fashion Design, FHNW, Hochschule für Gestaltung und Kunst (College of Design and Art). 1996–2002 Assistant Professor for the History and Theory of Architecture at the ETH Zurich (Institute gta). Publications, lectures, since 2005 Co-lecturer on interior design.

Marc Loeliger, born 1965, dipl. Architect ETH SIA BSA. Studies at the ETH Zurich, 1991 graduation, thesis with Prof. Flora Ruchat. Work for Meili & Peter Architects, Bétrix & Consolascio Architects and Peter Zumthor. Since 1997 independent work as architect, since 1999 Loeliger Strub Architecture with Barbara Strub, dipl. Architect ETH SIA BSA. 1998–2004 professorial assistant for design with Prof. Adrian Meyer, ETH Zurich. Since 2005 Professor for Design, since 2007 Professor for the Master's Course at the Center for Constructive Design at the ZHAW.

Jacques Lucan, born 1947, architect, Professor at the École polytechnique fédérale Lausanne and the École d'architecture de la ville et des territoires Marne-la-Vallée. Editor-in-Chief of the journal *matière*, published at the EPFAL, correspondant for *Casabella* and *werk, bauen + wohnen*. Upcoming book entitled *Le cycle de la composition, et après* to be published in 2009.

Christoph Luchsinger, born 1954, 1979 graduation from the ETH Zurich. 1980–1989 professorial assistant for Prof. André Corboz at the Professorship for the History of Urban Planning and at the Institute gta, ETH Zurich. 1989–1992 Professor for the History of Urban Planning, ETH Zurich, since 1990 architecture office with Max Bosshard in Lucerne. 1990 Editor of the journal *werk, bauen + wohnen*. 1995–200 Professor for Architecture and Urban Planning Analysis at the ZHAW, 1998–1999 Guest Professor for Design at the ETH Zurich, 2004 Guest Professor for Design at the Technical University of Ljubjana, Slovenia, since 2001 Professor at the Center for Urban Landscape at the ZHAW.

Martin Tschanz, born 1965, dipl. Architect ETH 1990, until 2001 professorial assistant at the Institute gta of the ETH Zurich. Exhibition and publications activity; Editor of the journal *archithese* 1992–1997, and *werk, bauen + wohnen* 2003–2008. Numerous guest teaching positions in architectural history and theory, since 2005 at the ZHAW Winterthur.

Christa Vogt, born 1974, dipl. Architect ETH. 2002–2005 work for Meili & Peter Architects, Zurich. 2005–2008 research assistant in the area of Research and Teaching at the ZHAW. Since 2008 professorial assistant with Prof. Andrea Deplazes, ETH Zurich. Independent work as architect.

Christoph Wieser, Ph.D. Dr sc., born 1967, dipl. Architect ETH, Architectural theoretician. Studied at the ETH Zurich and Lausanne, post-graduate work in History and Theory of Architecture at the Institute gta, ETH Zurich. Professorial assistant to Dr. Jean-Pierre Junker and Prof. Andrea Deplazes, both ETH Zurich. Dissertation at the ETH Lausanne on "The Expansion of Functionalism 1930–1950, with Examples from Switzerland and Sweden." 2005 Lecturer at the ETH Zurich and since 2006 at the ZHAW. Since 2003 Editor of the journal *werk, bauen + wohnen*, numerous publications.

Picture credits